After Magic

Moves beyond Super-Nature from Batman to Shakespeare

After Magic

Moves beyond Super-Nature from Batman to Shakespeare

by

Kester Brewin

ISBN: 978-0-9559813-9-5

For E and I

and all the magic they bring.

Huge thanks to Si for comments on the text.
Any remaining typos are entirely his fault. ;-)

'Sacrifice is the price of a good trick'

Borden — The Prestige

[I might be wrong]

Spoiler Alert

The plots of the following books and films are discussed in some depth in these pages - please be aware that the text may therefore contain spoilers. Familiarity with these works may be helpful, but is in no way essential.

The Tempest - William Shakespeare

The Tragedy of Macbeth - William Shakespeare

Harry Potter and the Deathly Hallows - JK Rowling

Jonathan Strange and Mr Norrell - Susannah Clarke

The Amazing Spiderman - directed by Marc Webb

Watchmen - written by Alan Moore, illustrated by Dave Gibbons

The Dark Knight Rises - directed by Christopher Nolan

The Prestige - directed by Christopher Nolan

American Splendor - directed by Shari Springer Berman and Robert Pulcini

The Usual Suspects - directed by Bryan Singer

(If you haven't yet finished *The Bible*, just to forewarn you: the hero dies near the end.)

Prologue

Magic is everywhere. Despite the best efforts of the Enlightenment and the pursuit of the scientific method to investigate our universe, stories about magic and fascination with magic have not only persisted, but blossomed. The most popular single volume fiction book of the past century, bar none, is the story of a hobbit and his adventures with wizards and a magical ring. The most popular book series has been that concerning a young wizard called Harry Potter. Not far behind is C.S. Lewis' *The Lion, the Witch and the Wardrobe*.

This is not a defence of the literary merit - or otherwise - of the fantasy genre, simply a statement of its deep roots in the popular imagination, roots that have grown and spread ever since stories have been told. *The Epic of Gilgamesh* and *Beowulf* are fantasy tales, and the ancient Greek fables of gods and fantastical journeys provide some of the surest foundations of all Western story-telling, direct ancestors of our modern-day superheroes like Superman and Batman.

Magic, fantasy and religion have been the narrative backdrop for all of human history, and, perhaps surprisingly in the world of the Higgs Boson and the fully decoded human genome, there seems to be no sign of waning interest in them - and yet belief in magic, *real* belief in forces beyond the material world around us, has collapsed in the past 100 years.

What are we to make of this? Most people no longer 'believe' in magic or even follow an orthodox religion and yet magical stories and superhero films abound. Is this simply nostalgia for a time when we did believe, or something else?

As these enduring magical stories plot out something of what it means to engage with the supernatural they also plot out how this supernatural engagement has affected the journey human beings have taken as we have come to understand both our world and our relationships with one another. My contention here is that the most long-lasting of these tales - the ones that go beyond familiarity and into archetype - all share a common strand as they come to fulfilment: they all contain a move *beyond* super-nature, a *renunciation* of magic in favour of something greater. It is by these stories that we will be helped in our natural next stage of human development: to navigate our way in the world 'after magic.'

That we work out how to make this move is terribly important. As I write, the top stories of the day contain more revelations about widespread sexual abuse in parts of the church, news of arrests of religious fundamentalists wanting to wreak havoc through campaigns of terror, large media corporations having hacked into people's phones and paid off policemen to gain material for tabloid stories, and the bizarre tale of a t-shirt for sale on *Amazon* with the slogan 'Keep Calm and Keep Raping,' which was apparently created and sold entirely without human invention by a computer algorithm.

What unites these stories are the problems that we face when we are involved in large institutions or interacting with large networks. These systems present large demands on us, and can, as we see in the examples above, lead to actions by 'normal' people that are lacking basic human empathy or kindness. Yet this problem is magnified massively when applied to the religious domain because of the theoretically *infinite* demand that a god can place on believers.

Dostoyevsky famously pronounced that 'if God does not exist, everything becomes permissible.' Modern thinkers have turned this on its head and seen that this infinite demand of the existence of a transcendent God can - and has been - used as a way of justifying inhuman behaviour, giving divine assent to violence and the bloody exercise of power. Dostoyevsky's formulation is thus inverted by recent philosophers to something like 'with God everything is justifiable.'

There are hard truths here. The pressures of work, the demand of a capitalist society for us to create profits at all costs, the dogmas of religious truth and the ecstasies of religious experience – all of these demands, from the 'very large' to the 'infinite' can lead us quickly into behaviour that looks very like delusion or madness, and is certainly less than graceful or kind. Yet we continue to live under these various demands either because we like security and cannot see any other way or simply because we find them addictive and tempting. They offer us meaning, purpose, power and wealth.

I am convinced that in our love of power and influence we have ignored the subtle move that many stories take in renouncing magic at their conclusions. My argument in this book is that we need to listen to them. This may sound like a strange idea. Aren't these just good stories? Sure, they hold our attention and make us think, but shouldn't we be turning to more serious sources to fund our thinking on such serious issues?

It's my strong belief that some of our greatest thinkers, philosophers and theologians are our great writers, film-makers and dramatists - yet they are also the least tapped and most ignored. We are foolish to underestimate the power of their vision and the richness of their teaching. The great artists – in whichever form or genre – are without exception those who best interrogate the human condition. Philosophers and theologians do the same work but come at the problem head-on, often resulting in sore heads and bloodied noses. Instead, as the great poet Emily Dickinson wrote:

Tell all the truth but tell it slant,
Success in circuit lies,
Too bright for our infirm delight
The truth's superb surprise;

The job of the artist is no more than to tell the truth, but at a slant - and it to these 'slanted' sources that these pages very deliberately turn, partly to inspire others to begin to see the great mass of serious and insightful thinking that lies beyond academic tomes.

What follows is a journey through the work of artists like Shakespeare and Christopher Nolan in the hope that we can explore something of what they have unearthed of our humanity, and thereby uncover a faithful re-reading of Christianity that follows their moves 'beyond super-nature' to something far, far greater. Beyond the religious domain, I want to propose that such a reading of Christianity will present not only a move beyond the problems of the infinite demands of an actually-existing god, but a way of dealing with the 'very large' demands placed on us by the 'big other' systems of capitalism, politics and technology that we have to interact with too. The hope is that by immersing ourselves in these stories, and accepting this radical re-reading of the Christian narrative as a model of life 'after magic,' our humanity will be restored and our addiction to power and violence broken.

But we have ground yet to cover before reaching that place; we must begin at the beginning, some 400 years ago in London, with news of a storm, and a ship feared lost at sea.

The Tempest

Where was he when he heard the news? Probably not in a tavern - he'd skirted round the edges of them as a younger man making his way, but seen talented friends fall in disputes over the reckoning, and others sunk so low by drink that few had grace to pull them from London's stinking gutters. He might have been rehearsing with his company, or writing for one of his patrons; perhaps, like all of us who have ploughed the page, he was stuck for an idea and waiting on his muse.

Then, through the door, a messenger, or friend, bringing news from the docks. Information had not yet left the hand and travelled only as fast a man could take it - as fast as a horse could be ridden or a ship sailed. In likelihood weeks would have passed since the actual event, and yet here was a boy running, spreading urgent word to Mr Shakespeare as quickly as he could carry it: the *Sea Venture*, the flagship of the Jamestown Company, of which Shakespeare was a shareholder, was ship-wrecked.

A storm. A tempest. A whirling wind had stirred in a far-off place. Perhaps the breeze lifted some of the parchments lying about the room. Disorder, disturbance.

Later, more news, and later still a verbal account from a survivor: for days the entire crew and passengers, gentlemen, slaves, women of ill repute, craftsmen, traders, merchants - all - regardless of status - had battled with the storm to bail out their leaking vessel. It had been put to sea too quickly, and its timbers hadn't properly sealed and now, split from the rest of the flotilla, it was sinking and breaking up in a huge hurricane. They had done all they could and, having seen their common humanity in their fight for life, had decided to go down together as brothers and sisters, breaking open the stores of rum and drinking each one's health.

Then land had been struck.

The *Sea Venture* had hit Bermuda, an island of plenty. Shipwrecked, they gathered ashore and found themselves in paradise. Fresh water, fresh fruit, easy hunting. And since they had bailed together, might they not now live together, and begin a new utopia? The slaves who had been aboard clearly wanted it so.

As I outlined in my previous book *Mutiny!,* those who had enjoyed the trappings of status and power over others had too much to lose from this new brotherhood, and too much to gain by pushing on to the Jamestown colony, where there was money to be made. Their commercial interests were a demand too great to ignore. Violently reinforcing the old social order, the captains and merchants forced the slaves to rebuild their own slave-ships, and left paradise behind, setting sail for a colony that they had no idea was destitute and close to death.

Who knows what Shakespeare made of the financial implications of this dramatic episode at sea? He was a wealthy man who had built up a fortune and was likely already thinking of stepping away from London to return to his hometown of Stratford-upon-Avon. Yet, whatever monies he had lost through his failed Jamestown shares, he had gained a kernel of an idea: a storm conjured up to bring about a shipwreck, shaking down the established order of things...

The Tempest, written just a year after the *Sea Venture* was wrecked, is widely regarded as one of Shakespeare's finest plays. It was likely the last full text that he wrote on his own and thus stands as something of a swan-song, the wise reflections of a man about to step away from the stage and retreat from the worlds that his stages had played. In *The Tempest* we find Prospero, a man who was once an Italian duke, but is now long ship-wrecked on a far-off island with his maturing daughter. Prospero uses the magical art he has learned to whip up a storm and to the island on that storm is carried Prospero's brother Antonio and the King of Naples. Many years previously, with the King complicit, Antonio had usurped Prospero as Duke of Milan, and now Prospero intends to use magic and trickery to restore his daughter to her rightful high position.

This he does, but the play has fascinated students of Shakespeare for centuries because the play ends with the perhaps surprising sight of Prospero giving up this 'rough magic.' Once he has put the world straight he renounces it and determines to break his magic staff and sink his magical texts in the sea:

> *Have I given fire and rifted Jove's stout oak*
> *With his own bolt; the strong-based promontory*
> *Have I made shake and by the spurs pluck'd up*
> *The pine and cedar: graves at my command*
> *Have waked their sleepers, oped, and let 'em forth*
> *By my so potent art. But this rough magic*
> *I here abjure, and, when I have required*
> *Some heavenly music, which even now I do,*
> *To work mine end upon their senses that*
> *This airy charm is for, I'll break my staff,*
> *Bury it certain fathoms in the earth,*
> *And deeper than did ever plummet sound*
> *I'll drown my book.*
>
> Act 5, Scene 1

In this people have seen parallels in Shakespeare's own life. He was about to break his staff - his quill - and put away his books too. He had done enough magic, and in the riches he had gained for himself through his plays had secured a high future for his beloved daughter.

Yet, having seen *The Tempest* performed last year, just as my last book *Mutiny* was published, I became aware that Prospero's act of renunciation recurs in countless other stories too. So many films and books I have seen and read have carried within them this same archetype: the hero lays down his 'potent art' at the conclusion of the piece.

It is to this pattern that I want to turn these pages because I am convinced that Prospero's act stands in a terribly deep tradition, one so powerful that it resonates through film and literature and right into the heart of what it means to be human.

More Fully Human

Why does Prospero lay down his magical art? Shakespeare, quite rightly as dramatist, does not provide a definitive answer and the question has remained for us to ponder, opening as it does a way into reflecting on Prospero's deeper drives.

At the surface level his abandonment of his powers signals to the audience that a new, more stable state has been reached. It is a 'happily ever after' moment because, now satisfied with the way things lie, Prospero sees no further need for supernatural intervention. Indeed, it is possible that Prospero considers the destruction of the means of his magic as vital to the sustenance of the reconciled state that he has now achieved. To remain in possession of powerful books and a magical staff would present a temptation both to him - and others who come after him - to take them up again and use them not to restore equilibrium *with* others, but gain power *over* them.

Tricked and cast out of Milan with his daughter, Prospero is aided in his 'rough magic' by the spirit Ariel, whom he saved from entrapment by the witch, Sycorax. Once Prospero has brought the king and others to repentance, finished his work of restoration and regained his status, he sees no need to carry on with magic.

> *'They being penitent, the sole drift of my purpose doth extend not a frown further.'*

Prospero delivers this line to Ariel at the beginning of Act 5, and in it we see that Prospero feels he has done just enough: now that they are penitent, he need not push things any more. He thus releases Ariel from his service and renounces magic. Yet, digging a layer deeper into the play, more complex motives for his renunciation emerge.

Firstly, while Alonso, the King of Naples, is fully repentant, Antonio, Prospero's brother never explicitly is. Frustratingly, there *is* no full reconciliation in the play. In other words, the magic that Prospero does *just about* works, but doesn't quite get things all the way to a satisfactory conclusion. Why then does he not persist with his potent art, and move to bring Antonio to repentance too? The eminent Shakespeare scholar Stephen Orgel has explored this question and notes:

> *Prospero's devotion to his secret studies is what caused all the trouble in the first place. [...] If he has now learned to be a good ruler through the exercise of his art, that is also what taught him to be a bad one.*[1]

Prospero admits as much himself. Antonio had motivation enough to try to get him cast out of Milan because his immersion in magical thought had turned him into a poor duke. The magic had been part of the problem; Prospero uses it carefully to bring his brother and the King to his island, and thus set up the conditions within which reconciliation can occur, but his long isolation has made him wise enough to see that if he is to be a decent ruler he must be so *without* resort to magic. The play does not show us the reconciliation between Antonio and Prospero - and perhaps there never was one - but Shakespeare is being clever here: he directs the audience (many of whom would have been men in power in London) to understand that the work of peacemaking must be

---

[1] Orgel, S., *Prospero's Wife*, in *Rewriting the Renaissance: Discourses of Sexual Difference in Early Modern Europe*, Chicago University Press, 1986, p 60.

completed in person, without higher agency, and that this work is 'outside' of the scope of the script - it is something the audience must leave the theatre and achieve themselves.

This is what resonates through the closing speech of the play, the epilogue that Prospero speaks to the audience alone:

> *Now my charms are all o'erthrown*
> *And what strength I have's mine own,*
> *Which is most faint: now, 'tis true,*
> *I must be here confined by you,*
> *Or sent to Naples. Let me not,*
> *Since I have my dukedom got*
> *And pardon'd the deceiver, dwell*
> *In this bare island by your spell;*
> *But release me from my bands*
> *With the help of your good hands...*

It is, in the end, only the audience who can complete the work of redemption and, by their own hands, release Prospero to be the good man he now knows he can be through his own strength alone. *'By renouncing his special powers,'* Orgel suggests, *'he becomes more fully human.'*[2]

Magic got Prospero into deep water and distracted him from his duties to his fellow people. In its abandonment he bravely returns himself to being simply a man with no special powers, yet in doing so enhances his humanity and opens the possibility of serving others well again.

---

[2] ibid., p 61.

Caliban and Ariel

At the surface level Prospero renounced magic because he saw that he no longer needed it. He had achieved what he had set out to do, and further use of his potent art risked disturbing the fragile reconciliations he had achieved.

Underneath this we now see that magic had in fact long been a destructive element in his life. It was not just that he gave up this positive force because he had no need of it, but that he needed to distance himself from it because the demands he had experienced under it had become a negative force. The move 'beyond the natural' had somehow poisoned his relationships with his peers and subjects. It was only in exclusion that he was able to reflect on just how severely his potent art had damaged his situation. He used it one more time – but only up to bring things to a certain point. His last trick brought about reconciliation with those further from him, but he was careful to leave it at that. Restoring his relationship with his brother had to be a face-to-face endeavour.

As with all good theatre, and Shakespeare in particular, we find multiple layers in the drama. Most obviously there is a surface level of dramatic action that must keep the audience rapt: every play needs to be driven by a decent plot. Then there is the secondary level of drives within the characters that respond to their own subconscious relationships with the rest of the cast. This is what we see in Prospero's reflection on the relationships he has had with his brother. Finally, however, there is the deeper level of the archetypal: that which impacts on the audience's response to the play within their *own* desires and actions outside of the theatre. It is at this deepest level that we now examine Prospero's actions, because it is here that they begin to move beyond the stage and speak to our own experience.

As Shakespeare's last play *The Tempest* stands as his parting thoughts on the human condition. Historical context is important here. In the early 17th century the human soul was still considered divided into three Platonic elements: the vegetative, the sensitive and the rational (which can be broadly paralleled with Freud's later classifications of the id, the ego and the super-ego.) Shakespeare weaves each of these elements into the cast, and thus the piece plays out as a narrative about the human struggle for wholeness.

Prospero is not alone on his island. He is joined by his daughter, who represents his 'future self' - one who can carry the play beyond curtain-fall into the next, unseen story - and Ariel, the spirit. He is also there with Caliban, who is coarsely written by Shakespeare as a base native, the son of the witch who tried to capture Ariel. Caliban has, like Ariel, become a servant of Prospero, but hates him for deposing him as the effective ruler of the island.

There are effective and important post-colonial readings and critiques of Shakespeare's characterisation of Caliban in the play, but it is not within the scope of this piece to deal with them now. Instead I want to consider these three characters who surround Prospero from the psycho-spiritual perspective that Shakespeare's world understood. Caliban is a symbol of Prospero's 'vegetative' nature - his base, organic physicality that is understood as fallen and in need of great discipline. He is Prospero's servant, yes, but is a troublesome and irascible one. Caliban is Prospero's shadow. Ariel, on the other hand, presents Prospero's 'sensitive' side - his spiritual, super-materiality.

In Freudian terms, Caliban is the id - the core instincts, and Ariel the super-ego - which acts as a higher conscience. This new model shows us Prospero as the rational (in Platonic terms) ego (in Freudian) who struggles to control his higher and lower drives. In some productions of the play this struggle has been made explicit with Prospero, Caliban and Ariel all played by the same actor, bringing to the fore the conflicts that lie within Prospero himself. The 'tempest' in the play is thus not so much the *meteorological* storm that Prospero creates, but the *psychological* squall that is going on within. It was this inner conflict that saw Prospero banished from Milan as his unhealthy interest in magic and magical books took him away from his responsibilities to others. Now, with a storm bringing his brother and the king back into his world, he must show that he has managed to calm the gales within himself, that he has achieved harmony between his id, ego and superego.

Prospero has dived deeper into magic in hope of finding some binding wholeness through it, even though it was dabbling in magic itself that led to his being torn apart. This is a rough and potent art that promises unity of self. Yet it not only blows the self apart the deeper one explores it, but offers itself as the route to wholeness - if only one will go that step further. Magic, in Prospero's world, has become a psycho-spiritual addiction, one that he must be rid of and bury deep, lest others be destroyed by it in future.

His daughter Miranda, for one, begs him to do so:

If by your art, my dearest father, you have
Put the wild waters in this roar, allay them.

And it is perhaps for his daughter - representing the hope of a better future - that Prospero acts. Indeed, his political machinations in the play seem less set on bringing about his own restoration to duke than on helping her into a marriage that steps away from the feud he and his brother have fought.

At this deepest level magic is presented as a force that Prospero has engaged to try to control a psyche that is wildly fragmented. He is torn between Duke Prospero and the caring father, an angry ex-Duke and a skilful manipulator, and the play plots the end of his attempts to use magic to unify these warring elements into a harmonious whole person. The breaking of his staff and burying of his books are the radical gestures that prove his turning away from the dark arts that have ripped him to shreds. His immersion in these arts had splintered him, and characters had formed legions within him. It was time to walk away, to renounce his powers and return home. Thus Prospero leaves himself in our hands, and his author, Shakespeare, puts down his quill, slips out from the crowds of babbling characters he has conjured, and returns to Stratford to live out a quiet life with his daughter.

Standing alone *The Tempest* grips and thrills, but it is only when its deep themes are seen to recur that we become alerted to the fact that that is not just one story but part of an archetype. This is what makes *The Tempest* all the more remarkable: not its uniqueness, but the fact that the themes within it are found resonating in a children's book of magical adventures some 400 years later.

Hallows

At the end of seven books JK Rowling's hero, Harry Potter, finally draws into his possession three powerful magical objects - the *Deathly Hallows* that give the title to the final instalment of the series. A perfect invisibility cloak, the 'resurrection stone' and the Elder Wand were long thought of as belonging to myth but, through his mentor Dumbledore's hints, Harry realises that they do exist. He is convinced that they are the only way to defeat his nemesis, Lord Voldemort.

Uniting these three Hallows should bring the wizard who owns them immense power and Harry has already proved himself capable of shouldering that without the vanity or pride that would corrupt lesser magicians. Yet Harry does something remarkable: he takes the Elder Wand and vouches to place it inside Dumbledore's tomb, thus putting it eternally out of use.

> *Harry held up the Elder Wand, and Ron and Hermione looked at it with a reverence that, even in his befuddled and sleep-deprived state, Harry did not like to see.*
>
> *'I don't want it,' said Harry.*
>
> *'What?' said Ron loudly. 'Are you mental?'*
>
> *'I know it's powerful,' said Harry wearily, but I was happier with mine. So...'*
>
> *'I'm putting the Elder Wand,' he told Dumbledore, who was watching him with enormous affection and admiration, 'back where it came from. It can stay there. If I die a natural death like Ignotus, its power will be broken, won't it?...'*

By placing the wand - also known as the Death Stick - in Dumbledore's tomb - deep into a place of death, Harry is ensuring that nobody will be able to kill him over it and thus become its new owner. His burying it, breaks it.

> *I'll break my staff,*
> *Bury it certain fathoms in the earth...*

Harry's friends are shocked, and in the film versions Ron tries to persuade Harry to let him have it instead. Yet Harry is adamant:

> *'That wand's more trouble than it's worth,' said Harry. 'And quite honestly,' he turned away from the painted portraits, thinking now only of the four-poster bed lying waiting for him in Gryffindor Tower, and wondering whether Kreacher might bring him a sandwich there, 'I've had enough trouble for a lifetime.'*[3]

Magic, it is quite clear from the Potter books, is both a blessing and a curse to Harry. It was a war over magical power that saw his parents killed, his godfather killed, Dumbledore and countless others killed, and it was this same internal war that saw him verge towards madness as his mind was sporadically linked directly to that of his arch-enemy Voldemort. Through dreams and visions his psyche became fragmented to the point of schizophrenia. Harry had no idea if he *was* Voldemort, or acting as the snake that Voldemort carried with him. He and this great dark wizard seemed to share some powerful connection, each mind able to see into the other. And yet, at the same time, Harry also had a special link into Dumbledore too. As a young wizard Harry was uniquely given access to the Headmaster's study and given

---

[3] Rowling, JK, *Harry Potter and the Deathly Hallows*, Bloomsbury, London, 2007, p. 600

individual lessons by him, trusted to be taken on special missions.

We are thus back with Prospero, Caliban and Ariel. Harry is a boy at war within himself, at the centre of a huge tempest that whirls through both the 'muggle' (non-magical) and magical worlds. Above him, in the higher place, is Dumbledore, 'the greatest wizard who ever lived,' and below him Voldemort, a base and foul wizard who has crawled back into reanimation through the floor of some far-off jungle.

At the beginning of the books Harry is unequivocal: on finding out that he is a wizard with magical powers, he is exultant, utterly delighted. This is the best thing that has ever happened to him. Magic will solve his problems and bring him escape from the terrible world that he lives in. He is taken to Hogwarts School, and nothing could be better: all is well, and the magical world is idyllic. However, this utopia soon reveals itself to be a less than peaceful place. Indeed, it is as if Harry's arriving at Hogwarts somehow triggers a gradual collapse of the magical world into chaos. It is only when Harry arrives that Voldemort begins to stir again and, as the series of books progresses, magic presents itself as darker and more conflicted than Harry could have ever imagined, placing on him an increasingly heavy series of demands.

Once again magic initially presents itself as the panacea, and is then revealed as the heart of the problem itself. Harry is so deep in though that only one last piece of magic will present him with the chance to move beyond it. Exiled, troubled and alone, with his baser and higher selves combining in the mental visitations of Dumbledore and Voldemort, Harry becomes increasingly isolated. He decides to return to Hogwarts, as if inviting upon himself the dark tempest. By this move he puts himself in a position to face his demons, having gathered the three 'Hallows' - these strongest magical objects - into one place.

However, just as in Shakespeare's play, the magic itself is insufficient. Though Rowling seems to present them as the locus of power and the only route to destroying Voldemort, the three Hallows in reality *don't* do anything to directly bring about his downfall. The invisibility cloak is useful and helps Harry gather information about Snape, which helps him *understand* his mission, yet it is itself invisible when the true last battle occurs. The resurrection stone helps Harry gather courage to meet Voldemort and to face his death, but Harry very deliberately drops it deep in the Forbidden Forest - *buried certain fathoms in the earth* – and thus it is lost forever. It's power was, ironically, to help Harry to overcome fear of dying, not to aid him in resurrection. As Harry comes face-to-face with Voldemort, it is Voldemort who actually holds the last Hallow, the Elder Wand. Tension builds as they prowl around each other, preparing to duel, Voldemort convinced that his possession of the Elder Wand will guarantee him victory. In fact, unbeknownst to him, the Elder Wand recognises Harry as its rightful owner, so, while it does function in Voldemort's hands, it doesn't carry any extra potency. At the climax, they both cast spells simultaneously, Voldemort - known as a boy as Tom Riddle - issuing a killing curse, while Harry opts for a disarming spell:

> *'Avada Kedavra!'*
> *'Expelliarmus!'*

> *The bang was like a cannon-blast and the golden flames that erupted between them, at the dead centre of the circle they had been treading, marked the point where the spells collided. Harry saw Voldemort's green jet meet his own spell, saw the Elder Wand fly high, dark against the sunrise, spinning across the enchanted ceiling like the*

head of Nagini, spinning through the air towards the master it would not kill, who had come to take full possession of it at last. And Harry, with the unerring skill of the Seeker, caught the wand in his free hand as Voldemort fell backwards. Tom Riddle hit the floor with a mundane finality, his body feeble and shrunken, the white hands empty, the snake-like face vacant and unknowing. Voldemort was dead, killed by his own rebounding curse... [4]

Voldemort is not directly killed by any of Harry's magic, nor by the Deathly Hallows: he is killed by his own curse rebounding on him. And yet, even with this, Harry understands at this point that magic has been insufficient. Prospero saw it too: magic could get him so far, but it could not bring about reconciliation with his own brother. Something deeper than magic was needed. Something like love.

In the very first chapter of the first book of the series, Harry Potter is presented to readers as 'The Boy Who Lived.' Voldemort had tried to kill him before, but the curse had rebounded then too. Voldemort hadn't died that time because he had protected himself from death by splitting his soul, but the reason why Harry hadn't then died is much later made clear: his mother's love had protected him. By laying down her life in love for her child, she had conjured a protection so much deeper than any magic. Voldemort, so mired in dark magic for so long, his 'snake-like vacant face' disfigured like that of an addict, was unable to experience this love, and was thus destined to remain unable to kill Harry.

---

[4] ibid. 595

By the time we reach the last chapter of the last book - seven volumes later - we find Harry grown up, some 19 years after he has killed Voldemort, waving off his own children to Hogwarts School of Witchcraft and Wizardry. Yet, oddly, in this final chapter Harry does *no magic at all* - perhaps the only chapter in the entire series where this is the case. His old friend Ron confides that he used a 'confunding charm' on his driving test examiner, but Harry is silent in response, and they fall to talk of dinner parties and growing families. He has had 'enough trouble for a lifetime,' and comes across as the picture of domesticity - the very thing he had hated his Uncle Vernon for throughout his childhood stay with him and the rest of the Dursley family. Magic arrived with a promise to take him away from the suburban boredom of the Dursley's home in Privet Drive, but then utterly blew his young life apart, taking him to the point of madness and mental breakdown, before he was able to overcome it and return to love.

It is this same love-beyond-magic that drew Prospero away from his own potent art for the sake of his daughter. It is this same love of a parent for a child that has bound Harry together and kept him intact during all of his troubles.

It is this love, not some wand or cloak, that was the real Hallow. Yet sometimes the love that exists is not strong enough to draw people out of the magic they have become embroiled in and when this happens things, sadly, tend to end in tragedy.

The Darkness

Three years before the Harry Potter series was concluded, Susanna Clarke published *Jonathan Strange & Mr Norrell*, described as 'unquestionably the finest English novel of the fantastic written in the last seventy years.'[5] In this remarkable book, Clarke imagines England at the turn of the 19th Century, and a 'gentleman-magician' called John Segundus who wonders to his polite society of York magicians why, despite all their meetings and study, nobody has actually tried to *do* any magic. One of the York club has heard of a recluse called Mr Norrell who apparently has been heard to perform genuine magic, though most believe this is nonsense. Segundus, however, finds Norrell, who agrees to perform magic in public at York Minster one Christmas night in 1806. He does so, to frightening effect:

> *The world had changed while the magicians had been inside the Church. Magic had returned to England whether the magicians wished it to or not.... Mr Segundus felt very tired by his adventure. Other gentlemen had been more frightened than he; he had seen magic and thought it wonderful beyond any thing he had imagined, and yet now that it was over his spirits were greatly agitated and he wished very much to be allowed to go quietly home without speaking to anyone[6].*

Unwillingly, Mr Norrell and his magic are brought to London, to the centre of society, and once again - just as with Prospero, just as with Harry Potter - the introduction of magic

---

[5] From the review by Neil Gaiman

[6] Clarke, S. *Jonathan Strange and Mr Norrell*, Bloomsbury, London, 2005, p. 41

initially presents itself as a delight. Ladies at dinner parties are wowed by his small acts and Norrell becomes hugely popular, even helping the government with grand illusions that help them win sea battles against the French. However, things take a dark turn when Norrell is called upon to bring the wife of one particular gentleman back to life. In doing so he strikes a pact with an ancient spirit, and very quickly the peaceful equilibrium of England is thoroughly disturbed.

Norrell is by nature an introvert who treasures his grand library of magical books and determines to stop anyone coming into possession of any significant texts by buying them up himself. Yet he is eventually persuaded to take on a young pupil - the vivacious and talented Jonathan Strange. Strange is an extravert and wants to open magic up for everyone. Norrell allows him to study his books, but Strange goes far deeper into them than either bargained for. Both are caught up in an increasingly dangerous and addictive cycle that drags them further away from normal reality and pulls many of their acquaintances down into a horrible parallel world where death dances at a permanent and joyless feast. Norrell and Strange are both terrified and yet unable to draw back from the Pandora's box they have opened.

Eventually Strange's beautiful wife is also kidnapped by the spirits that he and Norrell have unleashed from the magical underworld and the novel climaxes with Strange's mission to rescue his wife and be reconciled to her. As we now expect from the archetype we are in, it becomes clear that the only way to do this will be to perform one final piece of magic, and to do so from a place of deep exile. Caught inside a towering cloud of permanent darkness, Strange does manage to save his wife by killing the an ancient magical King, John Uskglass – a battle that brings about the destruction of much of Norrell's library. Together, Norrell and Strange end the book fighting for their sanity, their minds having been fractured and unhinged by their unleashing of magical power into an unsuspecting England.

As we know from the archetype, Strange's one last act of magic will not be *quite* enough. It brings his wife back to life, but cannot draw him or Norrell out of the permanent darkness that rages round them. Strange has done everything he can for her, confessing that '*it hurt me more than I could bear to think of you under the earth. I would have done anything - any thing at all - to fetch you safely out.*' And yet he is still stuck.

We know now from *The Tempest* and *Harry Potter* that it is loving sacrifice that will make that last step beyond magic, but, tragically, on the last page, Strange and his wife appear unable to take it:

> *They looked at each other for a long moment, and in that moment all was as it used to be - it was as if they had never parted; but she did not offer to go into the Darkness with him and he did not ask her.*[7]

It is a heartbreaking end because, even after all that they have been through, and the damage that magic has done to them, even with all of this, Strange and his wife appear unable to reach out to one another in that way of sacrificial love. Instead, with great sadness, Strange reverts to magic:

> *"One day," he said, "I shall find the right spell and banish the Darkness. And on that day I will come to you."*

> *"Yes. On that day. I will wait until then."*

---

[7] ibid.1006

He nodded and seemed about to depart, but then he hesitated. "Bell," he said, "do not wear black. Do not be a widow. Be happy. That is how I wish to think of you."

"I promise. And how shall I think of you?"

He considered a moment and then laughed. "Think of me with my nose in a book!"

They kissed once. Then he turned upon his heel and disappeared into the Darkness.

In the light of *The Tempest* and the story of *Harry Potter*, these last lines of *Jonathan Strange & Mr Norrell* become some of the most affecting in all of literature. Here is impulse to do magic exposed for what it is: a deepest, darkest cloud of depression. And here is our hero, who has been through so much to bring his wife back to the really existing world and yet, at the very last, he will not renounce that which has brought him so much trouble. He will be remembered as a man with his nose in a book, still convinced that he can conjure one last spell to dispel the Darkness, unable to see that the act of his wife stepping into it with him, a selfless act of love and devotion, would have melted it at once.

Strange's refusal to go beyond super-nature, to push through into life 'after magic' has terrible consequences. He will not drown his books, or give up his potent art, insisting instead that the magic that got him into this trouble will somehow get him out of it too. It cannot. The love that would have banished the Darkness and seen him reconciled to his wife was right there in front of them, but neither appeared able to make the sacrifice: Jonathan to take his nose out of his books, nor Bell to walk with him in his Darkness, if only for a moment. Thus, in this beautiful but ultimately heart-breaking novel we see the flawed, incomplete version of the archetype that *The Tempest* sets up: where our heroes cannot move beyond super-nature they are destined to remain in a cycle of recurring troubles. The demand that magic placed on both Norrell and Strange was too much. Enslaved by this potent art, they ended up giving up wife, family, community and happiness in service of it. Promising to make them great men, successful and significant, it gutted their humanity and kindness and drove them into dark exile.

It is to this struggle to remain human in the face of super-nature that we now turn, and to a man who deliberately borrowed the form of the bat, a creature rarely seen outside of the darkness.

Batman and Bane

Harry Potter and *Jonathan Strange & Mr Norrell* aside, there are not many fantasy books that break through into the artistic mainstream. As the best selling pre-Potter series of books of any genre the *Lord of the Rings* trilogy did way more than just that, producing record-breaking films too. In Tolkien's books we see once again that the central magical object - the ring of power - is one that needs destroying. It appears in *The Hobbit* as little more than an interesting trinket, a useful device to get Bilbo Baggins out of a difficult corner. However, as the books go on, we see it's destructive, corrupting and addictive nature. There are those who claim it should be saved and used to unite the different races of Middle Earth, but Gandalf - who as a mirror to JK Rowling's more fallible Dumbledore knows how much he will be tempted by it and stubbornly refuses to touch it - insists that it has to be destroyed. It is only once the ring is destroyed that humanity returns to those who had lived in its dark shadow for so long.

From ancient Shakespeare to modern fiction magic, perhaps counter-intuitively, is again and again portrayed as a destabilising force. Under the surface of magical classics we see warnings about addiction and messages urging the renunciation of super-nature. In each of the examples we have explored our hero is caught in a storm between good and evil, light and dark - between their higher and lower natures. In each case magic, despite having been part of the problem, continues to offer itself as the solution, as a way of binding up this chaotic psyche and bringing it under control. Yet choosing magic inevitably makes things worse and dehumanises the magician: they are torn apart inside and tempted into a morally questionable abyss. At each tale's conclusion it is the matter of the renunciation of magic and the sacrifice of powerful magical objects that governs whether the protagonist will truly become a hero. When they give up magic, their humanity is enhanced. Their heroism is not measured by the *use* of magic, but by their *abandonment* of it.

The arc of these stories can be summarised thus:

- A protagonist experiences a very human difficulty, perhaps a troubled childhood or lack of fulfilment;

- Magic presents itself as the solution to this difficulty, an opportunity to step out of the natural and solve this problem using super-nature;

- The magic proves impossible to control, and unleashes a tempest of far greater difficulty, perhaps in a fearsome nemesis;

- The protagonist is taken to the edge of sanity by this magical power, and dehumanised by it;

- Yet, with one last trick, the protagonist is able to arrive at the place where they can, by the abandonment or destruction of the magic that had wooed them, bring about a restoration, both of their world and within themselves;

- In doing so they become a hero, not for their acts of super-nature, but for their renunciation of this super-nature when it mattered. Their heroic act is located solely in their humanity, and particularly their sacrificial love for a companion.

We shouldn't be surprised that humanity is diminished by the engagement of super-nature and enhanced by the sacrifice of it, for magic is the conduction of a force that is beyond the natural, beyond the realm of human reality.

The stories we have looked at so far were all written as part of the British literary canon. In the United States, perhaps because of its Puritan roots, magical literature has been more suppressed. However, the same archetype exists, not with wizards and magicians, but in the realm of superheroes.

The first proper superhero story was *Superman*, published in 1938. At less than 100 years old the genre is thus still youthful and it is only recently, with the release of such comic strips at Alan Moore's *Watchmen* and the recent re-workings of the *Batman* and *Spiderman* franchises (and, at the time of writing, *Superman* returning as *Man of Steel* in early 2013) that it has approached maturity. What is clear from their genesis in the original *Superman* is that superhero stories are intimately tied to traditional America and its strong religious roots. With the son sent to earth, growing up incognito but finally emerging to save it, the original *Superman* film has been recognised to have key parallels with the Christian gospels - and with the 'nerdy' Clarke Kent, with traditional caricatures of Jewish culture too.[8]

The narrative arc of these early films follows a set pattern: a protagonist discovers that they have super-powers and, after two set-backs (one minor, then one major), rises to defeat a grand enemy. This grand enemy is usually a mad scientist, and thus the battle between them and the hero is one of super-power vs. super-science, with the super-power always winning. Across the Atlantic, 'bad' science has always had to bow to 'good' religion.

In the course of the film the hero generally has to keep his super-identity secret, and yet it is with their super-identity

---

[8] See http://en.wikipedia.org/wiki/Superman_(film)#Themes

that the heroine falls in love. This presents a conundrum for the hero: it is only as their human form that love can truly blossom, but only in their super-form do they feel 'man enough' to win the woman's affection. But their love issues run deeper. Inevitably, the loved one comes into great peril, and the super-hero feels that it is only in their super-form that they can save them from this danger. Yet, paradoxically, the danger that the woman is in has been created by their involvement with the superhero - generally because the grand enemy has kidnapped her. The superhero saves the day, but then has to refuse full relationship with the one they love, knowing that their love will put her in danger again.

The pioneer, lonely superhero flies away into the sunset, his love unrequited, his human form embracing the woman yet consciously aware of his human inadequacy. As the credits roll we know that no final equilibrium has been reached: because love is unrequited, a new villain will emerge to endanger the one he loves once again, allowing the hero to save her - and deepen his addiction to this tragic cycle. The hero is experiencing the near-infinite demand of romantic love, and has to create regular new villains in order for him to be able to rise up in his super-form to sate his desire to impress this woman.

The recent 'mature' versions of these films have brought some more interesting dimensions to this standard plot. As with all genres, the road to maturity is generally the road from the external to the internal. In his huge work on the subject Christopher Booker explores how the external monsters of our childhood stories eventually become the internal monsters of our deep desires in the novels we read in maturity.[9] Similarly, the early superhero films present

---

[9] Booker, C., *The Seven Basic Plots*, Continuum, London, 2005

monsters - enemies - who were totally external and unknown to the hero. More recently the villains are almost without exception unmasked as one-time intimates of the hero, friends or close colleagues who have fallen and are seeking revenge. The monster has moved within.

More importantly, in the context of what we have seen from the magical works we have looked at so far, the recent superhero films reflect this intimacy with the super-villain by suggesting that the hero is ultimately responsible for the mayhem that they themselves end up saving the world from. We see this most clearly in the latest, more mature reworking of the *Spiderman* franchise (*The Amazing Spiderman, 2012*). Here, it is Peter Parker's own meddling in a restricted area of a high-level laboratory that he has cheated his way into that results in him being bitten by a super-spider and thus gaining his powers. The result of this illegal and rash action is to rush another scientist into mutating his own DNA in hope of restoring his lost arm. Turning into a savage and violent lizard, the scientist Connor battles Spiderman, and they lay waste to huge areas of New York in their struggle. Spiderman of course wins through, but the film can be summarised neatly as Peter Parker desperately trying to put right the waves of destruction he himself has unleashed. New York ends up thankful for him saving the city, but the thanks ought to be more hollow: if Peter Parker had not created Spiderman through his own tampering, the city would not have had to be saved by him in the first place.

This is the magical archetype all over again. Presenting itself as a simple and harmless enhancement of nature, tapping into 'good' super-power brings about horrible destruction because it simultaneously unleashes its 'bad' equivalent. Yet the 'good' powers then insist that they are the only way to bring the 'bad' under control, thus tying the world into an addictive cycle of dependence on the superhero - who is the very one who brought the super-villain in with him.

Put in different language, the creation of the super-villain is necessary for the creation of the demand for the superhero. It is as if the superhero, underneath the cape almost always a person with a deficit of love and affirmation in their lives, creates the super-villain in order that they might be given an opportunity to show how great they really are. It's a chance for them finally to be able to impress the girl and cover over their human inadequacies.

In the seminal comic book series *Watchmen* (which brought a very British sensibility to the American genre in the person of writer Alan Moore) we see the emergence of this cycle very clearly. At the end of the story, Adrian Veidt - a hugely wealthy businessman and self-made superhero, fakes an alien invasion of New York city by hatching a grotesque beast in the middle of the city, killing millions. As the other heroes (with varying degrees of special powers) confront him in his Antarctic hideaway, Veidt shows them the result of his plan: the US and Russia have climbed down from nuclear threats and are uniting to fight this new, common enemy. He has unleashed a supernatural violence so horrific that 'natural' conflicts between nations cease.

This vividly presents the equation on which superhero stories are based: the super-violence required to stop natural violence needs to outweigh it by some shocking degree of magnitude. The 'hero' effectively uses divine violence in order to stop human violence - creating an infinite demand and leaving the natural world forever in their debt.

Yet who is to say that this will be the end of it, or that more, even greater violence might not be committed again to sustain this fragile peace? Rorschach, the ultra-rational crime-fighter sees this clearly and demands that Veidt's actions be unmasked and the invasion exposed as a fake. *'Never compromise,'* he says, steeling himself against the others who have been persuaded to let the lie stand, *'not even in the face of Armageddon.'* As he marches away across the snow to let the world know the truth he is challenged by the super-human Dr Manhattan, who then vaporises him. Yet Dr Manhattan himself decides that this is not a world he wishes to be a part of any longer, and takes himself away to another galaxy.

In *Watchmen*, Alan Moore cleverly exposes the dark side of the deal that superheroes make with the worlds they 'serve.' This connects us back with the enduring problem of magic as a disrupting and damaging force that promises peace and reconciliation through the exercise of the supernatural, yet ends up creating huge, dehumanising demands and far more destructive than 'natural' problems at the story's genesis.

However, superhero films differ from the magical works we have looked at in one key regard: the narrative and emotional locus is not on the 'middle' character of Prospero or the 'low' of Caliban, but on the 'high' character of Ariel. Hence, as we come to consider Christopher Nolan's *Batman* trilogy in relation to the archetype we have set up, it is not Batman himself who we need to parallel with Prospero, but Gotham City itself.

Gotham has crime problems, this is quite clear, and Batman is welcomed as a caped crusader who can clean up the city when the police department are failing. But little does Gotham know what it has got itself into: the street-level villainy is nothing compared to the mayhem that is unleashed when Batman's enemies come to town. The higher calibre crime-fighter only invites higher calibre criminals, leaving

Gotham caught in the final film *The Dark Knight Rises* between the 'high' nature of Batman and the 'low' of Bane.

At the opening of the film, with Batman in retirement and Bruce Wayne a virtual recluse (loveless, needing affirmation), Gotham is pretty much at peace. But no sooner than Batman comes out of the shadows again does Bane, a super-villain, emerge too. Bane takes Gotham into exile: blocking every entrance and exit and holding it ransom with a huge nuclear bomb that will destroy the city. He then releases the criminals that had been locked up while Gotham was peaceful, who initiate a form of proletarian revolution, with mock trials of the rich and powerful. Gotham, in other words, is brought to the edge of total fragmentation and destruction by the war that is waging between Bane and Batman. Are they so glad to have welcomed a superhero now?

Of course, Batman saves the day and the city is saved. But what follows – and this is Nolan bringing the form to maturity – is Batman's own recognition that his presence in the city creates a near infinite demand and can only bring harm to it. Rather than Gotham renouncing Batman - something it had tried to do on many occasions (and in countless other similar superhero films the city turns on the hero and tries to expel them) - Batman takes the renunciation into his own hands: he fakes his own death as he drags the nuclear bomb out over the ocean. Batman thus remains a hero - a martyr, but removes the demand by removing himself from further interference in the life of Gotham. The film ends with Bruce Wayne spotted with his love in a café in Florence.

Importantly we don't see *Batman* moving elsewhere, but *Bruce Wayne*. Indeed, central to Gotham's future security and peace is the fact of their acceptance of Batman's death. The trilogy ends when Bruce Wayne finally sees the error of his ways. He had thought that by the exercise of technological super-power facilitated by extreme wealth he could save the city he loved. Yet his massively sophisticated weaponry and enormous expenditure ended up drawing out an equally well-resourced villainous power, and in the struggle that followed between them the city was destroyed.

The final shot of Wayne in Florence is the uncomfortable message that most superhero movies find too difficult to voice: it is only in the putting to death of the 'super' part of themselves and the embracing of the weak and awkward 'human' part of their psyche that they have always struggled with that the demand will be annulled and peace will come. The truly heroic act is the decision to act within the limited human envelope. The reason we see it so rarely is only because the continuation of the franchise demands that the superhero carries on…knowing that more destruction will come as another super-villain rises.

In this light some of the most interesting characters in superhero stories turn out to be the host cities themselves. To what extent will they put up with the supernatural within their midst? What costs are they prepared to endure - gutted buildings, broken bridges, collapsed metro lines, mass killings of their police force (with only the beautiful apparently fated to survive) in order to have a superhero at their service? How great does the demand have to become before the city refuses to honour it?

In the mirror of these superhero movies we cannot but see reflected back the reality of the battleground of fundamentalist religion in America: with suppression of gay rights, women's rights, with the fight to prevent standard scientific theories being taught in schools, with the burning of the Qur'an and the halting of any progress on the Israel-

Palestine question by the religious right... at what point does the cost of embracing the supernatural become too high?

Our error in examining these films is often to cast ourselves in the role of the superheroes, or to allow ourselves to cast others as the super-villains. Our politicians and generals try to draw inspiration from them, flying into fighting crime and waging war on terror... Yet our place is neither with Batman or Bane; our place is in the middle, as citizens of Gotham City. Our place is as those who need to make an informed choice about which powers we will allow to be unleashed in our midst, and what demands we will allow to be made on us.

The most heroic thing we can do is to give up on our childhood dreams of being superheroes, and to free ourselves from their addictive lure. We need also to let go of our hope that some other super-power – whether religion, technology or a political formulation – will bring eternal peace and equilibrium. Great institutions can do brilliant work, but the inescapable problem with our projection onto them of super-natural ability is the large, dehumanising demands that they create.

Like Prospero, we need to return from our exile, step back from the madness that the supernatural has inflicted and return to our humanity, with all of the mundane suffering and normal materiality that that entails. Like Bruce Wayne, like Clarke Kent, we need to destroy the capes and reengage with the struggle of our human form, to find mercy, pity, peace and love while we, as William Blake put it, wear the plain human dress.

The Prestige

Christopher Nolan remains one of film's most interesting storytellers and with *Batman Begins* in 2005 he dragged the superhero film out of naiveté - the fully external monsters of Christopher Booker's thesis - and into maturity, where the dark forces are more projections of inner conflict. His films have been highly praised for their rich ideas, which many in Hollywood thought viewers would simply not be interested in. (*Inception*, with its highly complex and interwoven dream narratives, is a case in point.)

Nolan scored another hit in 2006 with *The Prestige*. Here we are thrown into the world of Victorian stage magic, and introduced to two magicians with an intense rivalry. Angier, more of an aristocrat, is the technician, all about big stagecraft, costumes and lights; Borden, the working man, is quieter, darker, and performs almost without panache. *The Prestige* is very different from the other sources we have looked at because here there is no pretence at any genuine magic. Everything is illusion; indeed, in this world the person who believes in magic the least is the magician himself. As Borden says '*if people actually believed the things I did on stage, they wouldn't clap, they'd scream.*'

The question of whether Angier and Borden's audiences *actually* believe in magic is not important here. When you go to a magic show it is very unlikely that you go believing that genuine magical powers are going to be displayed. Yet nor do you go wanting to be shown how each illusion is done and for everything to be explained. In order to receive the gifts that it can offer the proper manner in which to attend a show of illusion is to *suspend your disbelief.* For a short while you leave behind the rational and enter completely into the world of the trick. A good magic show leads a willing audience into doubt about their normally firmly held belief that everything is just an illusion; it is this that is exhilarating.

At least, this is how *The Prestige* is set up, but, having set this scene, the Nolan then begins to subvert it. One of the themes he explores is what happens when Angier begins to wonder if Borden really *can* do magic. The answer is made clear: *actually* believing in magic paradoxically destroys the world of the illusion. It removes Angier from the theatre of the trick; moving from a suspension of disbelief to the beginnings of actual belief drives him to insanity.

At the beginning of the film Borden's assistant, played beautifully by Michael Caine, explains the basic pattern in every illusion:

> *Every great magic trick consists of three parts, or acts. The first part is called 'The Pledge'. The magician shows you something ordinary: a deck of cards, a bird or a man. He shows you this object. Perhaps he asks you to inspect it to see if it is indeed real, unaltered, normal. But of course...it probably isn't.*
>
> *The second act is called 'The Turn.' The magician takes the ordinary something and makes it do something extraordinary. Now you're looking for the secret... but you won't find it, because of course you're not really looking. You don't really want to know. You want to be fooled.*
>
> *But you wouldn't clap yet. Because making something disappear isn't enough; you have to bring it back.*
>
> *That's why every magic trick has a third act, the hardest part, the part we call 'The Prestige.'*

We will return to the importance of this three-part performance later - what is important to note here is the size of 'The Pledges' that Caine uses. Any two-bit street magician can make a bird disappear; what Borden and Angier are both pursuing is the ultimate prize: *the disappearance of the body itself*. The 'transported man' trick that they are both attempting is the holy grail of magic: how to make the magician himself disappear from sight, and then immediately reappear in another place.

Borden presents his version, which Angier initially thinks will be easily explained. Yet he finds himself utterly unable to do so, and is driven mad trying to find out what the trick is, or whether indeed Borden is using a trick at all. Perhaps he really does have access to higher powers? We are familiar now with the symptoms of this madness: Angier projects both super-hero and super-villain status on Borden, tempted to believe that he really *is* magic, and at the same time cursing him as a devil whom he hates more than any other.

As it turns out, Borden is very cleverly using a double. He has an identical twin brother whom he has kept secret totally secret in order to perform this trick, even going to the lengths of inflicting on his twin the same gunshot injury to his hand in order to sustain the illusion. '*Sacrifice*,' Borden says towards the end, '*is the price of a good trick.*'

Nolan's direction here is brilliant. One watches the film for the first time wondering how Borden is performing this trick, knowing that he *cannot* be performing actual magic, but tempted to believe that he might be. And yet, using the conjurer's fine art of misdirection, on second viewing you realise that Nolan hasn't hidden a single thing. It is all there - the twin and all - if you only have eyes to see it. Nolan even tells us this fact right from the start: '*Are you watching closely?*' are the first lines of voiceover that the audience hear.

Angier, in a frenzy and jealous of Borden's huge celebrity with this trick, cannot watch carefully. He vows to do everything he can to perform a version of the 'transported man' too and persuades Nicolas Tesla - the mysterious and brilliant engineer-scientist - to build him a machine that will help him do it.

Again, Nolan doesn't hide anything, and once Angier's method is exposed properly we see that his grim solution has been there on screen all along. Tesla's machine creates a clone of Angier each time the trick is performed, yet he cannot be sure if it is *he* who is transported or the clone. Either way, the clones - or his 'original' self - must be disposed of. They fall through the floor of the stage and are drowned in a sealed tank each night.

In both cases then, with Borden and Angier, we see that the pursuit of this greatest trick - the disappearance of the body - requires brutal violence. In both cases a man is submerged and the magician's individuality is compromised. In both cases, a man dies - one physically, one socially. In both cases there is a level of madness, a hint of the unhinged psyche - not even in the *use* of magic, but in the pursuit of the *illusion* of it. In both cases, with the high showmanship of Angier's performance, and the low simplicity of Borden's, violence is needed to sustain this illusion.

Sacrifice may be the price of a good trick, but the pay-off is in the adoration and awe of the audience. With the 'transported man' this adulation goes far deeper and moves into reverence and some foreboding. The disappearance of the body frightens us; we have a natural human fear of death, of what lies beyond the disappearance of the material. A magician I spoke at length with described the unease and anxiety of those at his shows when he stops a trick at 'the turn.' He has made something disappear, and in his refusal to bring it back there is a sense of a tear in the fabric of material reality. *Where has it gone?* The audience applaud at 'the prestige' not simply because the trick has been amazing, but also out of a sense of relief that natural order has been restored.

Borden and Angier's 'transported man' illusions take these emotions to the extreme. With 'the pledge' Nolan shows us the electric sense of anticipation at what is about to happen. Then, at 'the turn,' with the disappearance of the body, there is total shock. The crowd are dumbstruck. A man has disappeared. *But to where?* In this moment of the turn the audience are being challenged about the very foundations of existence, for if someone can simply vanish then the world, this world of day-to-day experienced reality, cannot be all that there is. But these questions can only be presented for an instant, for the power of the 'transported man' trick is that the body reappears almost instantaneously in another place - an impossible distance for the magician to cover in the time. There is confusion and bedazzlement at the speed at which 'the turn' becomes 'the prestige' and it takes a while for the applause to come. But when it does, it is rapturous.

A body has been returned to us.

Someone has been brought back.

But from...*where?* From death?

Magicians and Priests

Angier and Borden are both very accomplished performers and the interaction with their audiences, especially given the central place of death in their illusions, shows them in something approaching a priestly role. This is nothing new. In anthropological terms there is total continuity between magic and religion; it is thought that the separation only arose with the rise of monotheism.

At the heart of this separation is the question of attribution. The religious are concerned with rituals and worship around the force - personal or otherwise - that acts as conduit between the natural and supernatural worlds. Magic, by contrast, 'is unconcerned with establishing causality, only repeatability.'[10] The magician and the priest differ in this same way: both are concerned with opening channels beyond the material, but only the priest wants to denominate the creator or founder of that place and attach meaning to it.

There are, however, similarities between them. Priest and magician both exercise a gate-keeping role and both consider themselves 'special' by mediating between the natural and super-natural worlds. Both create demands on their audiences. In Harry Potter there is a whole 'Ministry of Magic,' whose business it is to control the magical world. Indeed, Rowling's entire plot focuses on the struggle over who should have access to magic and be able exercise magical power. In Voldemort's 'Death Eaters' we see the Pharisaic impulse exemplified: the desire for purity, domination and regulation.

---

[10] See wikipedia.org/wiki/Magic_and_Religion

The same struggle is shown in Susanna Clarke's novel. When Mr Norrell is first discovered he takes some persuading to come to London to perform his magic in public - he initially sees no reason why magical work ought to need an audience. However, he soon becomes aware not only of the social influence his powers give him, but the power struggles going on with those around him who themselves want to control what company he keeps.

There is undeniably a similar attraction in the priestly role: to just enjoy closeness *to* a god, but control *of* a god - deciding who should get access, and how. Connectedly, part of the priest or shaman's role is thus to convince their audience that they need to keep coming back: it is in their interest to bring to the fore the infinite demand that a god's existence makes. In more familiar terms, in order to keep the church viable there would be no point blessing the congregation once and telling them that's it. The priest preaches a message of commitment and regular worship because they need to sustain the demand.

For magicians the three elements of the trick work to forge a form of dependency. Presentation, disappearance and reappearance – 'the turn,' 'the pledge' and 'the prestige' - are a circular journey that takes the audience to a place where they want more. To finish on the turn - as the magician I met testified - leaves people disturbed and unfulfilled. Something has gone - and one can't just keep on making things disappear. As Angier and Borden knew when they performed the 'transported man' illusion, the pledge, turn and prestige cycle applied to the disappearance and reappearance of a human being generated a very strong cycle of addiction, a large demand. These two men had special powers that made them indispensable: only they could make the body disappear *and* then make it reappear again.

For the Catholic priest, this same cycle exists in the central ritual of the Mass. Here the trick is not the 'transported man,' but the 'transubstantiated god.' In 'the pledge' we have the presentation of very ordinary, familiar and material elements - not a man this time, but some bread and wine. Then we have 'the turn,' where the elements are taken into the priest's hands and symbolically lifted out of sight into heaven. (It is from the Latin form of the liturgy at this point - *Hoc est corpus meum* - this is my body - that we get the magical words 'hocus pocus.') The elements have 'disappeared,' and yet the congregation remain unmoved from their pews. It is only at 'the prestige,' when they are returned to earth turned into the body and blood of Christ that those gathered respond en masse and go to consume this supposed flesh and blood. Borden's words come back to us:

> *If people actually believed the things I did on stage, they wouldn't clap, they'd scream.*

If magic is unconcerned about causality, only repeatability, then the Mass, with its emphasis on divine meaning and the requirement of regular repetition, is the perfect bridge between the often-separated spheres of magic and religion. In the person of the priest we have someone dressed in robes who is, for the purposes of the illusion, suppressing their identity. Under the surface of both the 'transported man' and the 'transubstantiated God' tricks are extremely violent murders from which the audience remain protected.

Yet there are important differences too. Because magic like that of Angier and Borden doesn't seek to interrogate the source of this higher power that they are tapping into, the audience remain dependent on the magicians for little more than their entertainment and thrall. The demand is not so high. However, with the Mass, the addition of deep meaning and eternal personal consequences encourages a full psycho-spiritual dependence not just on the divinity behind the ritual, but the priest performing it. The demand becomes infinite.

For Angier and Borden to create the illusion that they were 'higher' beings who had accessed super-nature they both, in their own ways, had to descend into the gutters of their 'low' natures too and commit horrible acts of violence. For them to be seen as gods, they were required to act like devils. This is exactly what we have seen before. Prospero has no choice: to benefit from the power of Ariel, he must also suffer the ignominy of Caliban. Harry cannot just have Dumbledore; relationship with him comes at the cost of resurrecting Voldemort. Gotham cannot welcome Batman without unleashing Bane.

And so it is within the 'transubstantiated God' too. With 'the prestige' in the Mass - with the return of the divine food as Jesus' actual body and blood - the congregation enter the addictive cycle that we see in the magical archetype: accessing super-nature (Our father in heaven...) comes at the price of raising a super-villain (deliver us from evil...). And yet, because through the priest God is now presented as the *only* one who can perform this final prestige, this great return of the body from the place of death, the faithful experience the infinite demand and are tied into a continuing cycle. They need God to be assured of protection from the evil that brought death into the world - despite this devilish super-villain having been created by the very same move that saw the superhero welcomed too.

Gotham called on Batman to solve a minor crime spree, and found itself plunged into a hellish exile from the rest of the world. Could it not be that perhaps ancient peoples called on gods to answer very human questions like insecurity and the workings of the natural world, and found themselves plunged into a guilt-ridden hell of original sin requiring an ultra-violent atonement?

At the centre of this addictive cycle by which an infinite demand is created is the priest-magician who, for different reasons, requires the illusion to be sustained through repetition. The priest performing the 'transubstantiated god,' or the magician performing the 'transported man,' having presented the audience with a conduit into super-nature, thus find themselves in a tricky position. As Angier and Borden knew, any revelation of the workings of the illusion, or any doubt cast upon it, threatened their status and position. People must believe 'the pledge' upon which the rest of the trick is based, and those who refuse to do so, heretics or sceptics who threaten the world of the trick, must be dealt with lest the whole show be ruined.

Macbeth

For magicians Angier and Borden the risk of exposure threatened only their own livelihoods. For those in the priestly role, or the monarchical role that saw itself as the divinely appointed head of a nation, disbelief in their power and prestige had far more serious consequences.

The question of how to deal with those who refused to tow the line that the dominant power structures of church and state reeled out is nowhere better explored than in another of Shakespeare's plays, *The Tragedy of Macbeth*. Written just four years before *The Tempest* it again brilliantly exposes the corrupting effects of magic and power, but also plays a subtle trick on the audience, leading them perhaps to question the way that evil power was attributed to the marginalised and vulnerable.

Macbeth was probably written to be performed to King James I, ostensibly as a way of making him feel more secure as monarch. Yet Shakespeare was never one for blind fawning and, as with *The Tempest*, the third, deepest, subtext of the play is as subversive as anything he wrote.

James' anxieties about his claim to the throne were well founded. Parliament had gathered round Elizabeth I encouraging her to execute James' mother, Mary Queen of Scots, with calls of 'kill the witch.' James clearly didn't want to be seen 'as a Scottish interloper, son of the scarlet whore of Babylon,'[11] and Shakespeare did not want to offer him the impression that he agreed. To this end Shakespeare wrote

---

[11] Greenblatt, S., *Will in the World - How Shakespeare Became Shakespeare*, Pimlico, London, 2005, p. 333

Macbeth with subtle allusions to the ancestor James liked to be thought connected to - a Scottish knight called Banquo who was believed to have helped bring about a coup and depose King Duncan. In Shakespeare's retelling of this 'history,' Banquo is murdered, but a son remains - and it is this son who becomes king, and sets off the line of accession to James. The surface level message of the play is thus simple: James is, like Banquo, a hero, and one worthy to be in a long line of kings.

Famously though, the play begins with three witches, and this sets the tone for the entire piece: dark, troubled and brooding. This is not a play whose text can be taken in cold light, and by using the witches Shakespeare is effectively announcing that there are deeper meanings behind the mists.

Having opened with the witches, Macbeth and Banquo come across these women in the third scene and hear a set of prophecies: Macbeth will become Thane of Cawdor and then king, and, though Banquo himself will not be king, his offspring will be. What follows is a morality tale about different responses to prophesy, to the demand that a voice from beyond places on us. Once a prediction is heard from the supernatural, to what extent do we have any freewill to follow it? Beyond the surface level of providing assurance to James, at this secondary level *Macbeth* is thus a play about how to act in response to the demand created by super-nature.

Macbeth himself is immediately captivated by the witches' pronouncements and from then on in exists in a kind of spell conjured by them. He immediately turns inward, not voicing ideas to others but speaking 'aside' to himself, to his inner thoughts. He believes that what the witches have said is his fate and thus his freewill is now compromised. He sees the great prize in front of him: he is to become king! But in order to reach these heights, he ends up plumbing the most awful, murderous depths. In a now-familiar pattern his experience of a demand from 'the beyond' turns him from a warrior into a madman, spiralling ever more horribly into hallucinations, paranoia and obsessive compulsion. Having gained the prize that he feels, through the witches' prophesy, is his divine right, he feels anything but a king:

> I had else been perfect,
> Whole as the marble, founded else as the rock,
> As broad and general as the casing air:
> But now I am cabin'd, cribb'd, confined, bound in
> To saucy doubts and fears.
> Act 3, Scene 4

Having taken the witches at their word, Macbeth is now a man savaged by doubt and fear. The nobleman Angus says of him:

> 'Now does he feel his title hang loose about him, like a giant's robe upon a dwarfish thief,'

Those about Macbeth see clearly how he has lost his mind, but he is addicted and returns to the witches to seek further assurances of his title. No more the innocent this second time, he is immersed deeper and deeper, and rather than clearer words all he gets is more darkness, more confusion - and yet, terrifyingly, more justification for the crimes that he has committed.

The Shakespeare scholar Stephen Greenblatt writes of Macbeth that 'it is a general principle of Shakespeare's tragedies that when the hero gets what he wants, the result is devastating.[12]' In his comedies, it is the opposite: when the

---

[12] ibid. 335

villain (temporarily) gets what he wants, calamity strikes, and the only ending the play can have is when the hero's desires are fulfilled. Why? Because they are good desires, for good things. The reason why devastation comes when the hero gets what he wants in a tragedy is because the drives of the hero are misplaced. As Greenblatt continues:

> 'Macbeth wins a great battle for his king, Duncan, and is handsomely rewarded, but the honor only whets his restless discontent. He kills Duncan and seizes the crown, but the treason initiates an unending nightmare of suspicion and anxiety.'

Macbeth feels that his discontentment will be quenched by the intervention of the witches, but his pact with their words opens up a whole battery of horrors. As in *The Tempest*, Shakespeare is presenting the pitfalls of tapping into the world of magic. We began by hearing that 'by renouncing his special powers [Prospero] becomes more fully human,' and see now that in the blind acceptance of the witches' powers, Macbeth becomes dramatically *less* human. Why? Because in him we see a perfect storm of insecurity and discontent, mixed with a belief that his fate has been predestined in the heavens, and is unalterable. He gives in to the infinite demand. This paradoxically results in Macbeth taking the matter very much into his own bloody hands: if he is fated to be king, then he has the divine right - he sees - to act with the brutality required to make that happen. As with all despotic tyrants the revision of Dostoyevsky's formulation comes back to us: 'with God, everything is justifiable.'

Banquo, on the other hand, is more circumspect about the witches' words. He too is promised great things - that his descendants will be kings - but he is wary of the dangers of taking them to heart:

And oftentimes, to win us to our harm,
The instruments of darkness tell us truths,
Win us with honest trifles, to betray's
In deepest consequence.
                                    Act 1, Scene 3

Macbeth is won with an 'honest trifle': after the witches predict it, he is announced Thane of Cawdor, though, with information meandering as it only could hundreds of years ago, his promotion by the king might well have already been heard by the witches through some natural channel. However, on their words, he becomes convinced that their other words must also come true, bringing very deep consequences indeed. Banquo, in contrast, lets the witches words lie and will not be turned by them. Unlike Macbeth, he speaks plainly to those gathered, not aside and into himself. This is a mark of one who is not full of discontentment, is not a house full of ghosts.

It is no accident that Shakespeare cast Banquo as the man unmoved by witches' words. Perhaps unsurprisingly given the way his mother was branded as a witch by the government of the day, James I was well known to be fascinated by witchcraft. He had even written a book on the subject - his *Daemonologie* of 1597 - that begins with these terrifying lines:

> *The fearefull aboundinge at this time in this countrie, of these detestable slaves of the Devil, the Witches or enchaunters, hath moved me (beloved reader) to dispatch in post, this following treatise of mine (...) to resolve the doubting (...) both that such assaults of Satan are most certainly practised, and that the instrument thereof merits most severely to be punished.*

Freud would have unsurprised to hear that James was a supporter of witch hunts and, in his reign as James VI of Scotland, took an intimate role in the North Berwick witch trials of 1590. He is known to have personally tortured Agnes

Sampson, who eventually confessed to being a witch and was burned. The trials were prompted by James' ship being blown off course to Norway on his return from Denmark. A Danish admiral blamed sorcery for the weather delay and, by the end of the witch hunt that followed, scores of women had professed involvement in dark arts.

None of this was uncommon in Scotland where it is thought thousands of witches were executed during James' reign. He wanted them dead because he feared their evil interference in his reign, as 'slaves of the Devil.' When he became king of England the hunts also moved south with him.

The England he inherited had vacillated between Catholic and Protestant leanings for many years, but with James' rising to the throne England joined Scotland as very much a Protestant-led state. With the reformation in the early 16th century - and the growth of Puritanism in England as a radical form of it - Catholicism was labelled as a deeply superstitious religion - the Mass was truly seen as 'hocus pocus' by Puritans. Yet many of England's leading families of the day were still deeply Catholic, and it was exactly around this time in 1605 that Guy Fawkes was set up as a Catholic stooge in a failed attempt to blow up the English parliament.[13] To join the dots: the rise of Protestant puritan power in England brought with it a connected rise in the need to rid the country of Catholic plotters against James and the witches who, as the Devil's slaves, were also seeking James' downfall.

---

[13] Many writers have puzzled over why Shakespeare never mentioned this plot directly in any play, especially *Macbeth*. The suspicion is that he, as one who had many Catholic sympathies and connections, didn't want to rock the boat unnecessarily. In these Puritan times it was difficult enough simply to be a playwright and actor.

In James' eyes these hunts against Catholics and against witches were one and the same thing. His persecution of those who didn't conform to his Protestant ideas of power and theology had both political and spiritual motives: his insecurity about his throne is based on potential Catholic schemers and evil witches who seek to dispose him. All of this would have been on Shakespeare's mind by the time he sat to write both *Macbeth* and *The Tempest*. Indeed, in this early 17th century it was a serious criminal offence to be 'recusant' - to refuse to attend a Protestant church.

James was not unusual in his outlook. For an anxious king threats could come from any side. This was before the dawn of the Enlightenment, when the workings of the supernatural were a profoundly important part of everyday life. Superstition was rife, and super-nature was often blamed for tragic early deaths, failed crops and many everyday deviations from the norm. Looking back now we can see it as a form of collective madness, a mass hysteria full of charms against the plague, the buying and selling of indulgences, the obsessive and competitive veneration of relics and the constant fear of God's punishment and the devil's possession.

So, while Shakespeare's casting of Banquo to represent James is, on the surface, an allusion to a mythic ancestor that will give James assurance that he is a rightful king, underneath that there is a subtle challenge to James for here was a king who was petrified by the supposed power of witches - and thus far more like Macbeth than the coolly sceptical Banquo. At this second level of the play Shakespeare appears to be warning James: if you carry on living in fear of magic and witchcraft you are destined, like Macbeth, for madness and destruction. His play for King James reads initially like an assurance of the king's rightful place and then as a warning against seeing evil opposition under every flagstone. Finally, however, at the deepest level, it challenges the audience about the very nature of the witches who create the demand that provides the dramatic tension.

Macbeth deals with witches but, because of the context of the play being performed for James, people would have understood that Shakespeare was alluding to all those whom James demonised: Catholics, recusants, traditional village apothecaries - anyone who fell outside of the narrow confines of Protestant dogma. Shakespeare presents these women in *Macbeth* as grotesques. Their femininity is questioned by their facial hair and they are cast out from any normal social interaction, left to meet on dark, windswept heaths. This was a popular portrayal that remains still: witches are seen as fully degraded women, hags, ugly, shrieking, beset by warts and boils, friendly only with each other. It is because they are *so* exaggerated Shakespeare is asking the audience to think about the drives that push them into the creation of these caricatures, and the people who lie behind them.

Village women of these times were low status, and those who were poor and single were extremely vulnerable. As Greenblatt points out:

> *People could attribute catastrophes to natural causes as well, but an expected blow - a violent storm; a mysterious, wasting sickness; an inexplicable case of impotence - set them grumbling menacingly at the poor, ugly, defenceless old woman in the hovel at the end of the lane.*[14]

Under James these marginalised women were now perceived as a threat to the stability of the nation. Because of their poverty, because of their existence outside of society's

---

[14] Greenblatt, S., *Will in the World - How Shakespeare Became Shakespeare*, Pimlico, London, 2005, p. 343

norms, because of their distance from the church and its narrow view of family and community, suddenly - and terrifyingly – these women became open to accusations of being all that the church feared. Having simply been the oddball of the village, they now had super-villain status cast on them.

Just as *Jonathan Strange and Mr Norrell's* fictional reintroduction of magic into England brought about a collective madness in them and terrible destruction to the country, so the amplification of the supernatural that we see following the Reformation brought about a neurotic fear of witchcraft and evil that bordered on hysteria. Luther's insistence that people did not need a priest to represent them to God opened up the possibility of everyday people tapping into heaven. Yet this ripping open of the supernatural conduit meant the opposite could now also be true: everyday folk could be possessed by the devil. God's divine power to save by grace created an intensification in the power of the devil to destroy. Naturally, nobody wanted to admit that they themselves might have evil within, so in an act of transference we see the creation of scapegoats on the edges of communities who suffered this evil possession on their behalf. Who better to fit the bill in a church that was rich and male than destitute, marginalised women?

This is then the subversive subtext to *Macbeth*: the protagonist's move into super-nature, his willingness to go along with the witches, doesn't simply bring about a descent into madness, but also horrible persecution of 'the other.' Yet this persecution is actually an act of transference. James is the king of England, and thus represents the head that controls the English body; Shakespeare's warning to James - and Protestant England - is that his hunting of witches, and his willingness to see their workings everywhere, signals a demonization of his own shadow. Rather than facing up to its fears and dealing with doubt and conflict at the internal, human level, England under James projected it externally onto witches and attributed it to the work of the devil.

James wrote of the *'fearful abounding of these detestable slaves of the Devil'* and that he needed to *'resolve the doubting that such assaults of Satan are most certainly practised.'* Yet we know now that Bane and Batman, Voldemort and Dumbledore, Ariel and Caliban come inextricably together. James could not bring reformed theology to England without cost; he could not tear down the rood screen and free God from the priests' shackles without also unleashing a great fear of evil. In trying to expunge his own doubts about the assaults of Satan, he needed to find evidence of devilish activity. His fawning officials found it in *'the poor, ugly, defenceless old woman in the hovel at the end of the lane.'*

The witch becomes a vessel into which could be poured all of the things neurotic, Protestant England suppressed. In a church that saw sex as dirty and ungodly we see witches painted as satanic whores, practising terrible unnatural sexual relations. It is no surprise then that we see James I, a powerful and anxious Protestant, testing Agnes Sampson for witchcraft by tying her up and performing a close and intimate examination of her body. Church-sanctioned witch-hunter men would strip women, inspect their genitals and examine them for extra nipples. Their 'success' in discovering witches was no more than a violent exposure of their own suppressed sexuality. Puritans were not allowed to dance, so we see witches caricatured as dancing around cauldrons, giddy and high on emotion. Puritans saw the natural world as fallen, and needing man's redeeming labour, so in witches we see deep connections with earth and animals – women who can turn into cats, and spells that involve deep-dug roots and forest-deep grubs.

In casting the witches as grotesque, absurd caricatures Shakespeare is paradoxically willing us to see the real women behind them: women who were full of fear, marginalised and highly vulnerable. Perhaps they had had a child out of wedlock, or relations with a man who was not their husband. Perhaps they had been born with learning difficulties, or a physical abnormality. Accusing a girl of witchcraft was easy to do, but terribly hard for her to disprove, and in many witch trials we see tit-for-tat accusations by families in dispute with one another.

Macbeth stands as a complex warning to a king and country obsessed with superstition: listening to its demands will lead not only to madness, but, by projecting super-villain status onto them as scapegoats, widespread persecution of those on the margins too. If a nation is best judged by how it treats the weakest, this comes as a damning indictment of 17th century England.

James had plenty who fawned around him, but his Bard was never so dim. In the witches of *Macbeth* James was confronted with that which appeared to condone his beliefs, yet in the subtle subversion that was as much as he could afford, Shakespeare also made his points: he who hands his fate to super-nature will be taken through madness and brought down by it and, more painfully, those who are most vulnerable, those on the edges of society, the poor, the outsider, will be demonised along the way, gruesomely violated and often murdered.

Tragically, we still see this today. Fundamentalist religion still requires demons to be created in order to protect itself from having to come to terms with its own internal fears. Those who are gay, those who are Muslim, those who are immigrants, those who are disabled, those who doubt, those who are women, those who are black - through history each of these groups has become a demonised other. They have had super-villain status projected onto them, and special powers have been attributed to them. They steal our jobs. They destroy marriage. They are the devil's own spawn. They are whores. They are über-criminal. Yet each of these attributions comes, like James, only from the failure of religion to see beyond its fears, fears that are created by the move that diminishes its humanity through a caving in to the apparently infinite demand of super-nature.

Beyond *Macbeth* and into *The Tempest* Shakespeare showed how this humanity can yet be restored when his protagonists have the courage to lay down these undeniably 'potent arts' and see what comes 'after magic.' And yet, as we shall now see, this move of renunciation is the same one made at the very inception of the Christianity that James and others had so sourly twisted.

After Magic

The stories that we have drawn on come from different genres and different eras. The world within which Shakespeare was writing towards the end of his life could not be more different from the world in which JK Rowling was writing in the prime of hers. Yet stretching from Elizabethan theatre right through the superhero era and into modern-day fantasy novels for both adults and children we see the same pattern at work. Into lives where there is trouble, disappointment and dissatisfaction an opening from the super-natural presents itself as a powerful and swift way out. It offers the opportunity to step above the humdrum of the everyday world into an exciting new one, one that is ripe for re-discovery in the pages of ancient texts and the words of ancient seers.

Yet the universe demands balance, and in each story we have seen that it is impossible to open the gates of heaven without also unlocking the gates of hell. In trying to deal with the forces that they have unleashed the protagonists in each tale descend into madness. Where the new powers they had wielded initially appeared to enhance their humanity, bringing them status and influence, it then rapidly diminishes it, bringing thoughts of cruelty and violence as they crumble under its demands. They then struggle to empathise with the communities around them and end up demonising 'the other.'

In the 'dark' versions of these stories, the tragedies if you will, the protagonist fails to escape the darkness that they have created and their psyche fragments ever further as they fall towards social or physical death.

In the 'light' versions of these stories, in the comedies, the protagonists understand that there is a power *beyond* magic, *beyond* super-nature. It is a struggle to renounce the potent arts that have recreated them, to cast away the powerful objects and devices that have channelled this power for them, but, gathering them in one last flourish, they are courageous enough to do so. In this brave act we see their humanity restored and fulfilled and see that the true power beyond power was, is, always has been, love.

This love-beyond-power is not a romantic love for, as many of Shakespeare's other plays testify, that is a love that also presents itself as madness with its own large demands. Romeo's crazed actions, Viola's impossibly knotted cross-dressing love triangle... in these comic and tragic characters we see the love they fall into afflict them with all the symptoms of lunacy: narcissism, the willingness to do crazy things and blast through any obstacle in order to get their hands on the one they love. No, that is not the sort of love we are talking about. The love we see 'after magic' is a love that prefers others to the self. It is the great love that Jesus spoke of in the gospels, not the love that lays waste *to* others in order to lie with another, but the love that lays down its life *for* others.

It is the love Prospero has for his daughter and, I am positing, his brother - a love that knows that magic must have no further place in their relationships if they are to be reconciled.

It is the love Harry Potter's mother displayed for him in giving up her life to protect him - the same enduring, sacrificial, human love that we see in Harry that shows itself greater and more important than all of Dumbledore's and Voldemort's spells combined.

It is the love Harry shows as he walks defenceless into the Forbidden Forest to meet Voldemort, laying his magical powers aside as he lays down his own life - preferring to die if that is what it takes to stop others being hurt.

It is the love Batman - or, more accurately - Bruce Wayne - finally shows for Gotham City by laying down the 'super' part of himself for good, putting away his special weapons and leaving the city forever, knowing that this is the only way that Gotham will be safe and that he will be able to enter a fulfilling human relationship.

What should we understand from these stories - and the countless others that follow their pattern of renunciation of super-nature in favour of love? They have emerged over many hundreds of years, from different countries, and yet have settled themselves deep into our culture. Were they singular tales, or ones that failed to stand the test of time, we might do well to ignore them. Taken together they sing in persistent chorus, and when stories do this we ignore their message either at our own peril - or leaving others at the margins in greater peril still. Their endurance urges us to take them seriously; their breadth of audience - from anxious kings in the 17th century to growing teenagers in the 21st - urges us to allow them to speak to the deepest parts of our humanity, to the metanarratives that are the forge within which our culture in the West has been formed.

For us in the West, perhaps the key foundational metanarrative is that presented in the Christian gospels and expounded by St Paul in his letters. It is on the meaning of this story of supernatural intervention into human reality that so much of Western civilisation and thinking has been built. By the time William Shakespeare was writing *Macbeth* Christianity had moved far from it humble origins in the

Roman outpost of Palestine to becoming the issue on which countless bloody power struggles had been waged. For 200 years Christians and Muslims had fought in horrific battles in the Crusades, and for centuries since Catholics and Protestants have fought for political and theological dominance throughout Europe and much of Asia.

In the traditional telling of the story Jesus is presented as the divine superhero. As we now know the creation of this 'high' figure cannot occur without the balancing creation of a 'low' super-villain. Jesus fights for us in our battle with the super-villain and, in the final great scene, appears mortally wounded but returns resurrected to bring about a great victory. In this sense, Jesus' life, death and resurrection parallel the three parts to any trick: a body is presented that then 'disappears' into the tomb. Yet the grand 'prestige' is still to come - Jesus is resurrected, and we see the reappearance of the body.

In theological terms the result of this is summarised in Augustine's famous formulation: *'God became man [sic], so that man might become God.'* In historical and socio-political terms the result of belief in this has tended to be *'God became man, so that man might become inhuman.'* From Macbeth to Prospero to Batman to Jonathan Strange to Angier to Harry Potter we have seen that the move into magic, into channelling super-nature, leads to a diminution of humanity and to the demonization of 'the other.' This fictional archetype is repeated throughout the historical record of the church where we see endless stories of violence, sexual violation, hypocrisy, political machination, misogyny and systemic demonization of countless marginal groups. Are we seriously to believe that this is the faithful response to Jesus' sermon on the mount where he calls on his followers to love the other, to give humbly and avoid ostentation, to be merciful, to be peacemakers?

I want to contend that Shakespeare's challenge to King James - he of the great translation of the Holy Bible - is the same challenge that we are presented with today: what shall we do in the face of super-nature? Shall we accept its demands like Macbeth and be led blindly by it, walking that path to inhuman violence and persecution in pursuit of power? Or shall we have the courage like Banquo to resist?

In Christian terms Macbeth's interactions with the witches on the wild heath can be paralleled with Jesus' temptations in wilderness. Both are spoken to by voices from the beyond; both have positions of power and glory projected onto them. Macbeth hears these voices and is literally bewitched by them. He abandons his free will and descends into madness in pursuit of their fulfilment. Jesus, on the other hand, like Banquo, is sceptical about their message and refuses to be bound by the words he hears. Banquo's speech could equally have been spoken by Jesus in the desert:

> And oftentimes, to win us to our harm,
> The instruments of darkness tell us truths,
> Win us with honest trifles, to betray's
> In deepest consequence.

Macbeth is a tragedy because Macbeth himself fails to see beyond the world of magic. Are we to resign ourselves to Christianity being a similar tragedy? Considering much of the history of the Christian church it would seem reasonable to do so and, given the recent appalling stories of systematic abuse of children and the toxic fundamentalist Christianity that is so full of hate, it is no surprise that many have already consigned Christianity to the bin, seeing it as hypocritical and inhumane. Yet, while it is so tempting to do so, I am pained to follow suit for the simple reason that the character of Jesus is

67

so far removed from the character of the church that purports to follow him. Nor do I stand alone in this view. The atheist writer Philip Pullman brilliantly outlined the same dichotomy between Jesus and Christianity in *The Good Man Jesus and the Scoundrel Christ*. The agnostic aesthete Oscar Wilde, imprisoned in Reading gaol for homosexual acts, expressed his deep appreciation of Christ as the perfect artist in *De Profundis*, where he argues that:

> 'With a width and wonder of imagination that fills one almost with awe, [Christ] took the entire world of the inarticulate, the voiceless world of pain, as his kingdom, and made of himself its external mouthpiece.[15]'

Wilde's book is a cry for a community gathered around this different Jesus, and his cry has been repeated more and more in recent years by philosophers like Simon Critchley in *The Faith of the Faithless* and Slavoj Žižek in, for example, *First as Tragedy, Then as Farce*. These writers have both called for new political formations to crystallise out of the message of early Christianity, a message that precedes the later development of the Christian church that wielded so much power.

The church as it exists now might consider these moves to be a threat to orthodox Christian teaching. But where has this apparent orthodoxy got us? What I want to propose is that the pattern we have explored in so many great works over such a long period allows us to read anew the gospel narrative and see that the move beyond super-nature into love is one which is followed *by Jesus himself*. If this is right then this offers us a great hope, for orthodox Christianity is now not sited in the place of tragedy, of sublimation of our free will into the

---

15 Wilde, O., *De Profundis*, Penguin, London, 1954, p. 171

infinite demand of super-nature and thus a descent into madness and inhumanity, but in the place of triumph, of a move beyond super-nature into the greater place of sacrificial love and the fulfilment of what it means to be human.

As we know, the gospels begin in classic superhero style with a man born and raised in odd circumstances. Having searched around and asked those who know more than me, I still cannot find a superhero character who has living parents or a 'normal' upbringing. Batman's parents are dead. Harry Potter's parents are dead. Superman is raised by surrogate parents on earth, but his biological parents are dead. Spiderman's parents are dead. Iron Man's parents are dead. Captain America's parents are dead. Wolverine's parents are dead. Why is this? It seems that to place the superhero into the situation of being an orphan allows the narrative to draw in their superpowers more easily. Cutting the ancestral line means that our superhero protagonist grows up in a different way, and thus takes the story off on a tangent - rather than it simply following the lineage of parent-child- and onwards. The cut with natural biological family permits the grafting in of something super-natural.

When we come to Jesus, he too has this odd genesis - born to a human mother and divine father. Joseph is traditionally assumed to die before Jesus begins his ministry as he is never mentioned beyond the birth narratives, and Jesus effectively cuts any family binds in Mark 3 when he responds to information that his mother and brothers are outside looking for him with the words, 'who are my mother and brothers?'

Having been born, and then growing up, before he begins his ministry Jesus goes off to the wilderness to pray. It is *right* here - at the very emergence of Jesus' divine ministry - that we see the co-emergence of his super-villain. Before this point, before this moment on the cusp of Jesus' move from being baptised and called God's favoured son and into his ministry, there is *no* mention of Satan or the devil in any of the gospels. No Batman without Bane; no Jesus without Satan.

After this period of doubting his powers and the purpose to which he should put them - a rite of passage for all superheroes - Jesus 'goes public' and is initially welcomed with open arms. People cheer him and follow his every move. He is the solution to their problems, a messiah who will rid Israel – his Gotham – of the occupation they are under. However, as in all stories, those in law enforcement don't like him and feel undermined. Opposition grows, and there are initial skirmishes between Jesus and the law, and Jesus and his 'super-villain' the devil. The action builds to a final showdown involving the law, the super-villain and the superhero. There is a great battle and our hero appears to die.

What happens next is where we need to carefully reconsider the Christian story because, if we follow traditional Christian doctrine, we see a surprising departure from the archetype that we have studied. What we hear *preached* is that the hero dies, but, having defeated his super-villain, he is resurrected as the divine body and draws everyone into perfect heavenly peace. However, what we see *practised* is Jesus dying, rising from the dead and his followers developing a religion of power that is a very long way from any picture of peace and harmony.

I believe we can faithfully re-read the passion narrative so that it stays *within* the archetype we have developed, and thus leads us beyond super-nature and into love. Central to this reading is Jesus' divestment of his divinity – his renunciation of his 'potent art.'

As he moves towards his death Jesus goes to pray in the garden at Gethsemane. This is where we see Jesus at his most human, his most vulnerable. He pleads for another way other than the brutal execution he sees coming. We see blood and sweat and anguish, sleep deprivation and exhaustion. This is the physical Jesus, the one who calls himself not the 'Son of God' but, 81 times - more than any title he uses for himself in the gospels - the 'Son of Man.'

The anxiety of Gethsemane is the anxiety of the embrace of raw humanity. It is the final act, begun in prayer three years before in the wilderness, of stepping away from super-nature. He will face pain and do so as a fully human man, without recourse to divine succour, without the help of any godly assistance. The temptation Jesus faced in the wilderness was to become the superhero: to feed the people from rocks, to jump from the Temple. He knows the spectacle that this will cause, the huge surge in popularity, the clamour it will create. But he also knows the madness, the insanity of such a path and the demands it will bring: the constant need of the crowd to see more, to do it again, to do something bigger, and from there to them vying for control of him, access to him, co-opting him into their political agenda, pushing for him to use his power to empower. Gethsemane is the final overcoming of that temptation. He will not do it.

The bravest thing Bruce Wayne does is to strip away the hi-tech suits, the gadgets and advanced weapons, the wealth and adoration, cast off the 'super' part of himself and learn to exist in the world as his weak, fallible, human self. This, I propose, is part of the mystery of what Jesus does at Gethsemane. The Jesus we see met with a kiss and marched away from that garden, the Jesus who affirms himself as 'son of man,' is the Jesus 'after magic.' He will not lie under oath and deny his heritage, but neither will he wear that divine mantle and act on it. Soldiers and others mock him and demand that he prophesies. He refuses. He is crucified, and again those gathered mock him, saying that he should prove his divinity by saving himself. This, of course, would be the act of the superhero - to break the shackles and save himself and others from imminent peril. But Jesus refuses, his unadulterated humanity underlined by his desperate and perhaps regretful cry of abandonment by God. He is forsaken. He is a man. He will die.

Prospero's final words come back to us, as if from Jesus' own lips, nailed to a cross:

Now my charms are all o'erthrown
And what strength I have's mine own,
Which is most faint: now, 'tis true,
I must be here confined by you...

He is confined to the material earth, bound hard and fast to it. He thirsts, he cries out, exhausted, and dies. At his death the curtain in the temple rips from top to bottom and the ground shakes, opening up tombs:

Graves at my command
Have waked their sleepers, oped, and let 'em forth
By my so potent art...

Here are symbols of activity above and below: he has come from heaven, and, on dying, is now considered to have passed into Hades. Yet he refuses to be bound by either, and refuses to work any more miracles.

But this rough magic
I here abjure, and, when I have required
Some heavenly music, which even now I do,
To work mine end upon their senses that
This airy charm is for, I'll break my staff,
Bury it certain fathoms in the earth...

Why? Why do this? We know already. The renunciation of super-nature is done out of love. By killing off Batman, Bane is also removed. In releasing Ariel from his service, Caliban is also released too. In divesting himself of divinity, in entering fully into humanity, Jesus removes the infinite demand, draws the sting of both God and Satan, super-hero and super-villain. The move into super-nature carries with it such temptations of power that it drives people to madness, to inhumane violence, to demonization. God's forsaking of himself is the final act of self-emptying in order that those whom God loves might walk free.

After magic, Augustine's formulation is now revised again:

God became man so that we might become... human.

God saw that it was only by the emptying out of Jesus' divinity, only by the simultaneous shutting of the gates of heaven and hell, that we might come to human fullness. This was the love of the cross: to put God to death, to move beyond super-nature and sacrifice everything for love. Only by this might we avoid madness; only by this might we truly be able to love one another, and love each and every 'other.'

Let us be clear: this move is not one into atheism. The renunciation of magic is never about a denial of its existence. To live 'after magic' is to be fully aware of the perils of super-nature and how it can rip apart human relations, and to deliberately, out of love, step away. Magic could do many things, but Prospero came to realise it could not do one thing: it could not bring about reconciliation. This is why even God gives it up. In the greatest sacrifice, he steps down from divinity and becomes human, because it was within and among humanity that reconciliation was needed.

Where, then, does this leave the resurrection? For now it leaves it exactly where Jesus left it when he modelled it at the Last Supper. In the breaking of bread and drinking of wine the community of believers take within themselves a symbol of Jesus' body and blood. The act of communion is, like all good tricks, about *repeatability*. Again and again we see the three parts. 'The pledge' is made: this is my body, this is my blood. And 'the turn' is completed: the elements are consumed and the body disappears. *But this isn't enough. There always has to be a third act.* Where then is 'the prestige'?

Here is the brilliance of God, for in the physical sense the body is not returned: there *is* no miraculous prestige, no supernatural return of the body, and because of this the addictive cycle can be broken and the demand annulled. And yet... and yet... Prospero has not yet finished:

> *Release me from my bands*
> *With the help of your good hands...*

The prestige is revealed as none other than the work of the community. By breaking up, distributing and ingesting these symbols of God's death, *we* become the resurrected body of Christ - we become his 'good hands' materially at work in the world in which we live. The prestige is presented not as a supernatural return of the body, but as the material return of it as bodies working sacrificially, lovingly as a distributed material community.

The body returns not as the superhero to save Gotham, but as the communal spirit of public service that will be the only way that Gotham is saved.

American Splendour

Two years before Christopher Nolan dragged the superhero movie into psychological maturity, Shari Springer Berman and Robert Pulcini released *American Splendor,* based on the comic of the same name. The film begins one Halloween in downtown Cleveland as a group of children are out trick-or-treating.

> *'Well ain't that cute,'* a women comments, opening her door to the boys and looking along the line in front of her, *'all the little superheroes here on our porch. We've got Superman here, and Batman, and his sidekick Robin - and Green Lantern!'* She pauses at the end of the line, where a scruffy boy without any costume stands. *'And what about you, young man?'*
>
> The boy looks affronted. *'What about what?'*
>
> *'Who are you supposed to be?!'* the woman asks.
>
> He shrugs. *'I'm Harvey Pekar.'*
>
> *'Harvey Pekar? THAT doesn't sound like a superhero to me!'*
>
> Harvey shakes his head, exasperated.
>
> *'I ain't no superhero lady,*
> *I'm just a kid from the neighbourhood!'*

He walks off, head down, kicking out at the road as ghosts and witches carrying sacks of sweets swarm into houses along the road, beginning a film that charts his work creating a comic that, for once, was not based on a superhero.

Pekar remained in Cleveland all his life and worked for decades as a filing clerk in a local hospital. In his mid thirties he began writing down stories of his day-to-day existence - the monotony, the grind of work, relationships, illness, the difficulty of finding a house, getting on with family and colleagues. Meeting the groundbreaking illustrator Robert Crumb, Pekar began releasing *American Splendor* - a comic based on his observations - while continuing his menial job.

American Splendor quickly gained cult status and has been called one of the most compelling and transformative series in the history of comics. Way before blogs, status updates or any graphic novel memoirs, Pekar was documenting everyday life as 'the poet laureate of Cleveland.' *'Ordinary life,'* he liked to say, *'is pretty complex stuff,'* and standing in his own clothes, with no pretence at any superpower, Pekar represents the true heroes of modern life: those who graft at public service, committed to friends and determined not to be beaten down. *'Life is a war of attrition,'* he said in an interview in the Daily Telegraph. *'You have to stay active on all fronts. It's one thing after another. I've tried to control a chaotic universe. And it's a losing battle. But I can't let go. I've tried, but I can't.'*

This is the life Bruce Wayne will find back in Gotham once the mystique of Florence wears off - and if his hoards of money ever run out. It is the life of the everyday hero with limited resources but a steely determination to have a creative output and try to improve the lot of those around them. It is the life that Wayne will have to become accustomed to if he is truly committed to helping the city he loves. His exploits as Batman have shown quite clearly that the move into super-nature brings about terrible destruction - yet his courage to go beyond that and cast off his powers opens the door for hope that, through sacrificial love for place, he will do greater - if quieter - works of reconciliation and regeneration in future.

This speaks into the religious sphere too. All around London I see fly-posters advertising nights where God's great power will manifest itself and bring about revival in the supposedly god-forsaken city I call home. Charismatic men in sharp suits beam out from billboards promising healing, prosperity and great works of power if only people will pray harder and worship more loudly, drawing themselves into frenzies of loud singing and shaking, spouting 'thus sayeth the LORD' and speaking in ecstatic tongues, while just down the road in the Bethlehem and Maudsley Hospital (from where we get the word 'Bedlam') paranoid schizophrenics are sedated and have the voices in their heads calmed with cocktails of pharmaceuticals.

Batman, Superman, Billy Graham, Barack Obama-man... we project such powers onto these figures that we can only end up in disappointment. They will save the world. They will turn things around. They will bring us back to glory. And yet by the very act of projection of superhero status we inadvertently create equal and opposite super-villains too - Bane, Satan, Sarah Palin – a process that in turn demands the creation of a group who need to be demonised: the rich of Gotham, immigrants, Democrats, Republicans. The pressure we put ourselves under trying to prop up lives driven by the infinite demands of super-nature is immense, often driving people into madness as commitments to church meetings outweigh any duties to friends, doctrinal statements create internal clashes and inherited beliefs about supernatural intervention lead to indefensible claims of divine retribution in the face of terrorist attacks or climate events. Families are torn apart as pastors burn out and congregations churn, and politicians find themselves unable to run for office without making surface statements about deep belief in God.

Is it possible that a faith 'after magic' can help us to do any better?

As my own spirituality has gradually moved beyond the boundaries of what is traditionally accepted as Christianity, people within the church have demanded what the practical outworking of any radically different theological position might be. Isn't this all just philosophical naval-gazing, or masturbatory deconstruction? My strong belief is that the move beyond super-nature is not only a profoundly orthodox one, but one that also opens up into a practical manifesto for just living in the face of the demands of politics, technology and capitalism.

Faith 'after magic' renounces any divine succour precisely because this is what Jesus himself did. It does so in favour of love. Again, this is not a turn to atheism (nor a move into traditional liberal theology) but a deliberate turning away from pretence at divine favour. Seeing the descent into inhumane thought and practice that drawing on the supernatural seems to inescapably bring, faith 'after magic' refuses to attribute blame for illness either to the grand scheme of God or to the work of super-villains (and similarly refuses to praise God for the provision of parking spaces.) Instead, it boldly accepts the radical responsibility of being the only 'prestige' there is - of becoming the resurrected body of Christ, and thus living for all that the Son of Man stood for: justice for the poor, fair taxation, rights for women, love for the marginalised, great festivals, shared meals and freedom for the oppressed. Practising faith 'after magic' is to stand with the godless and the powerless - and to do so even without a thought of anything other than the human power of the love that we bring with us.

The question that has powered so many sermons and so many religious arguments is 'how should you live?' From acceptable styles of dress to acceptable styles of music, from who you sleep with to who you work with, the emphasis has been on lists of acceptable behaviours and practices that are unchangeable by human communities because they are ordained by God.

The Harry Potter books begin with 'the boy who lived,' and end with, in essence, 'the boy who loved.' Similarly, in place of the sermon on 'how should you live?' escaping from under the demand to worship and defer to commandments of supernature, faith 'after magic' asks simply this: 'how should you love?' Jesus is quite clear in the gospels: love for God means no more than caring for those in need around you. Two parables in particular speak to this.

In the parable of the good Samaritan we see this sort of love in action, practised by one considered a heretic by those of great religious standing who walked on by. This idea of the heretic acting as the one in the truly orthodox place is the very same idea that drove my previous book *Mutiny*. To complete the circle, pirates, I want to suggest, offer a model of living 'after magic.' These men were kept by princes and rich merchants as virtual slaves on their ships. They were brutally beaten and treated appallingly, having virtually no rights. They were expendable, replaceable parts in the emerging machine of global capitalism. Their turn to piracy was *not* about a turn to theft - every Royal Navy ship sailing the Atlantic was thieving too. The turn to piracy was about a courageous act of self-determination and a life lived outside of the near-infinite demands of those who oppressed them. Pirates were those who were fed up of having their lives controlled by forces supposedly higher than themselves. Pirates were those who refused to believe those in power over them who preached a message that the sailor's status as a filthy low-life was assigned them by God. Pirates were those who refused to accept that their reward would be in heaven - if they towed the line, accepted the whip and worked quietly now. Refusing these denominations, pirates turned on their oppressors and demanded that their individuality and humanity was recognised.

The symbol used to mark a sailor's death in the ship's log was a skull and crossed bones - the skull replete with tiny wings that allowed it to fly up to heaven. Pirates appropriated this symbol and summarily cut off the wings. Their sailing under this Jolly Roger made it clear: in their rebellion they had died to the systems of power, monarchy and religion that had violently oppressed them, but, in death, they refused to fly off to heaven. No, they would make their heaven here on earth by running their ships democratically, sharing resources fairly, offering compensation for injury, capturing slave ships and setting the slaves free.

In pirates we see a refusal to accept the labels that the powerful want to give us and a rejection of the demands put upon them. In pirates we see a smashing of the illusion that the name and position the powerful offer is the one God himself has given. The pirate's mutiny is a celebration of their humanity and this ability to see each person as a worthy human being - regardless of wealth, ethnicity or religion - is the beginning of a better world.

The pirate's radical self-determination, their refusal to have their identity and humanity diminished by the power of a 'big other' had religious, political and social dimensions. As recent news items have shown, it is not *just* in the religious sphere that we see abuse being covered up and brushed under the carpet, but in these other dimensions too. Individuals within political parties, armed forces, relief agencies and media organisations have been guilty of not speaking out, and these large 'incorporations' collectively guilty of both failing those who suffered and pressurising those who knew not to tell the truth. So the issue of human responses to being part of institutions is a wider one than religion – submission to authority and the power of corporations in a capitalist regime lead to good people into the madness of doing inhumane things to save their jobs and keep the peace.

However, it is to the religious sphere that we must eventually speak, because this is where the buck finally stops: the claims that religions make in referring to a *divine* 'big other' mean that those within these religious incorporations can feel an *infinite* demand to submit to authority and remain acquiescent. Pirates rebelled against their captains, but these captains served a monarch who in turn saw him-or-herself appointed by God.

This is why in the toxic religious climate we find ourselves in it may paradoxically be the most godly thing to do live as if god did not exist. This is faith 'after magic' and it is no more than the decision to take truly seriously Jesus own words in the second pertinent parable, found in Matthew chapter 25:

> *'I was hungry and you gave me something to eat, I was thirsty and you gave me something to drink, I was a stranger and you invited me in, I needed clothes and you clothed me, I was sick and you looked after me, I was in prison and you came to visit me.'*
>
> *Then the righteous will answer him, 'Lord, when did we see you hungry and feed you, or thirsty and give you something to drink? When did we see you a stranger and invite you in, or needing clothes and clothe you? When did we see you sick or in prison and go to visit you?'*

> *The King will reply, 'Truly I tell you, whatever you did*
> *for one of the least of these brothers and sisters of mine,*
> *you did for me.'*

Vitally, the people to whom these words were spoken had no concept that they were doing any of these things for God, nor even sought to do so. They were living as if God were simply not part of the issue, the divine demand reduced to the far more immediate demands of the poor among them. Their only urge to action is to love the other, and to do so with no thought for God's existence.

In 1995 Kevin Spacey played a brilliant role as Verbal in *The Usual Suspects*. The film is shot as a series of flashbacks as Verbal is interrogated by a detective, creating a story of a mythically violent criminal called Kaiser Soze. Towards the end of the film, Verbal is talking about the way Soze was said to function, and tells the detective, *'the greatest trick the devil ever played was convincing world he didn't exist.'* By the trick of non-existence the devil could go about the devil's business, unhindered by the problem of people working against his existence. Because the devil *didn't* exist, people had no need to concern themselves with doing battle with him.

What Jesus is saying in Matthew 25 is that God plays this trick too. By becoming incarnate ('the turn') and then dying into *non*-existence ('the pledge') God can continue to act even while *not existing*, unencumbered by the problems that would be inherent in existence, viz: the draw into madness, the imposition of an infinite demand, the demonization of the other and the parallel creation of a super-villain. How can God do this? Plainly by the community of believers becoming the 'prestige' instead: being the returned body of Christ who act out God's existence by feeding the hungry, healing the sick and visiting those in prison. This community that then gathers around the *absence* of God's patent *non-existence* is a brilliant trick because it avoids the infinite demand of God's *actual* existence.

It is a trick that the church has failed to play properly. By insisting that when it gathers as the body of Christ it gathers around some present, actually existing, divine entity, it simultaneously denies the possibility of the community becoming 'the prestige.' This then reduces the requirement of the community to act because the external god who actually exists can act instead. However, in believing in the existence of this supernatural being, it *also* creates an infinite demand on itself as servants of that god – and thus an impossible tension is created. (Additionally, when this body does act it risks offending those it seeks to serve who see in the church's actions ulterior motives and a desire to proselytise.) In doing this the key aspect of Jesus' message in Matthew 25 has been lost: those who work for justice should have *no conception that they are serving God*, because this is the only way to both achieve 'the prestige' – the return of the body to do sacrificial acts of love - while avoiding the pitfalls of super-nature.

From a philosophical standpoint my hunch is that the move I am suggesting - that the only godly life is the one where God doesn't exist - might ease us past the recent spat between two contemporary thinkers, the celebrated Slovenian philosopher Slavoj Žižek and the English academic and writer Simon Critchley. They have argued over the past two years about our ability or otherwise to act *at all* to make the world better.

It will take minds greater than mine to fully unpack the details of their opposing viewpoints, but my understanding of the argument is as follows. In Žižek's view:

The threat today is not passivity, but pseudo-activity, the urge to 'be active,' to 'participate,' to mask the nothingness of what goes on. People intervene all the time, 'do something'; academics participate in meaningless debates, and so on.[16]

Žižek's problem with this pseudo-activity is that it ends up validating the Empire, the 'big system' that is the cause of war and oppression. So buying a 'fair-trade' coffee from *Starbucks* simply perpetuates the system that allows a multinational like *Starbucks* to exploit people on low wages in the first place. His solution to the infinite demand of these huge systems:

The truly difficult thing is to step back, to withdraw. Those in power often prefer a 'critical' participation, a dialogue, to silence.'[17]

Žižek sees that large scale systems - 'big others' like corporations, capitalism or religion - risk placing these large or infinite demands on us. The pseudo-action that he is critical off acts like a release valve, appearing to critique or challenge these large systems, but really just assuaging our guilt at having been compromised by them. For Žižek, given that full destruction of the 'big other' is impossible, the only way to escape the violence of the infinite demand is silence and non-action.

Critchley has been vocal in his disagreement with this view, and the two men have traded blows through the pages of various publications. He has expanded his critique in his recent book *The Faith of the Faithless*, where he notes:

Žižek's work leaves us in a fearful and fateful deadlock. A deadlock both metaphysical or philosophical, and

[16] Žižek, S., *Violence*, Profile Books, London, p. 183.
[17] ibid.

practical or political: the only thing to do is to do
nothing. We should just sit and wait. Don't act, never
commit, and dream of an absolute cataclysmic,
revolutionary act of violence.[18]

Only this 'revolutionary act of violence' - the sort that
Adrian Veidt manufactures in Alan Moore's *Watchmen* - will
sort everything, once and for all. But one cannot imagine
Jesus speaking in Matthew 25, congratulating those who wait
on this divine violence on their withdrawal from action, letting
the hungry go unfed lest feeding them propped up the regime
that made them hungry in the first place.

Yet, on the other hand, Žižek is in many ways correct:
pseudo-actions such as buying fair trade froth *are* meaningless
as they fail to do anything to challenge the root of the systems
that continue to perpetrate violence and diminish humanity.
How can we bridge these divided opinions?

The power lies in the move Jesus makes in taking the
community gathered around him 'beyond super-nature.' With
his gradual yet deliberate divestment of his divine nature
Jesus is stripping away the infinite demand and the violence
and moral corruption that that can bring. With the
disappearance of this apparently divine body through what
appears to be the Žižekian 'cataclysmic, revolutionary act of
violence,' the demand is reduced to nothing. Yet, as Žižek
must know full well, even when such revolutions occur and
systems of oppression are overthrown what tends to happen is
that new, equally demanding ones appear in their place. This
has happened innumerable times in the religious and political
spheres, from the excessive violence of the Reformation to the
gulags of the Soviets.

---

[18] Critchley, S., *The Faith of the Faithless*, Verso, London, p. 213

But this is where the true kernel of Christianity is so radical, for what follows this disappearance of the body is not some transcendent 'prestige' – an act that would lead back to an infinite demand – nor the emergence of a vacuum into which some other infinitely demanding system might grow, but the dispersed, material prestige of the gathered community becoming the body that is returned. The power of this trick of extant non-existence is that the violent and dehumanising power of the infinite demand is removed, and yet in its place emerges a self-organising demand that is fully located in the gathering of the community.

Is this not what Jesus means when he speaks about being present 'when two or three are gathered'? This is not some magic trick of god becoming present, but rather the ongoing prestige of a gathered community willing to act and respond to the continuing demands of an unjust and hurting world. Thus Critchley's urge for practical and material actions is satisfied, while Žižek's insistence that the 'big other' is removed is satisfied too. In this way Christianity becomes not a personal salvation *by* an infinite God, but a salvation *from* all infinite and large demands – whether religious, political, social or economic. It transcends a narrow religious pattern to become a way of stepping out from the madness that super-nature brings and the violence that its demand perpetuates.

At a more mundane level - knowing this question may be coming from some quarters - if the godly life is to live as if God did not exist, should people continue to gather to go to worship in church? My own view, as I have expressed it in *Mutiny* and elsewhere is that the church as we see it actually existing now needs to die because they are places where people are led to believe that they are gathering around an actually existing divine presence. This opens the way to the kinds of problems already noted. However, if these sorts of churches were allowed to die then we could see ground cleared and Christian communities emerge where God once more did not actually exist. But what could this possibly mean? How could a supposedly Christian community then gather if the godly thing to do was to live as if god did not exist? How, in other words, could a community celebrate a life 'after magic?'

To answer this I would return to the idea of attending a magic show. People do not refuse to go to magic shows because they don't believe in magic. No. People go to magic shows even though they *don't* believe but, in order to receive the gifts that the magic show has to offer, they *suspend their disbelief* while they are there. To go truly believing in magic (and berating those who don't attend) would be insane, and to go to criticise a magic show as fraud would be to miss the point.

In the church 'after magic' might still see people gathering together, but doing so with the core belief firstly that they gather around an absence, not a presence, and secondly, paradoxically, gathering with in temporary suspension of disbelief about this absence in order to receive the gifts this has to offer.

As an aside, it is for these same reasons that I'd question the likely longevity of the 'atheist church' projects that have begun emerging recently.[19] I sincerely hope that they do very well – and absolutely the love the playful spirit within which they are being done. But to continue to gather around an a-theism week in and week out could, I suspect be too little to sustain a community, especially when those who are lonely, needy, hungry and hurting begin to attend too. What will be the reaction of those leading then? Will they be working out ways in which the community can genuinely care for people? I

---

[19] See, for example, SundayAssembly.com

hope so. But my hunch is that the very concrete absence around which they gather may make things unsustainable.

What I am proposing instead is that people living as if god did not exist gather, as in a magic show, to temporarily suspend their disbelief in god's absence. In this space they thus gather around a non-actually-existing presence. Why? Because this then fills the demand-vacuum at the centre of any community, but does so without the violence of an actual infinite demand.

The Christian living 'after magic' thus embraces this life of paradox that Jesus sets out in Matthew 25: the most godly life is that lived as if God does not exist, because only in this way can both the infinite demands of religion and the very-large demands of other systems be removed. 'After magic' the far greater power of sacrificial love comes to the fore, and with people drawn away from destructive cycles and a diminution of their humanity, there remains the material 'prestige' of the community as the absent god's hands who are willing to meet the demands of a needy world.

My personal experience of this has been to allow a huge sigh of relief - thank God we don't have to worry about the absurdity of God anymore! Faith beyond super-nature is releasing and visceral. It brings with it a sense of clarity and responsibility, of self-determination and the freedom to make a good future... and joy at never having to sing a bunch of choruses again. Yet I understand that for many the move to life 'after magic' will be a step out of comfort and routine that is simply too big. What is very clear is that it is not an easy option. This is not an opt-out for those who find Christianity too challenging or uncomfortable. Quite the opposite. Committing to love beyond super-nature requires the difficult renunciation of things that many around you may still hold very dear. Taking radical responsibility for your future rather than defaulting to 'seeking God's will' or moving unquestioningly through the ranks of the corporation you work for may precipitate changes in your life that will be costly and troublesome. But be very clear: any hypocrisy will slowly strangle you, and avoiding challenge will mean failing by default.

As she gave the commencement address to Harvard students in June of 2008, JK Rowling spoke about the powerful effect that failure had had on her life. Yes, she was now speaking as perhaps the world's most famous author, but back in the years before Harry Potter had taken her to that place she was a single mother struggling to pay her bills with a non-vocational degree that her parents had warned her would get her nowhere. She was suffering depression, trying to take care of her daughter, and everything around her said that she had genuinely failed. Yet she learned, she said, to see that 'rock bottom became the solid foundation on which I rebuilt my life.' She used her Harvard speech to make a plea for these greatly privileged students to work to improve the world they were now entering. In doing so, she quoted the Greek author Plutarch: *What we achieve inwardly will change outer reality*, commenting as she concluded:

> 'We do not need magic to transform our world; we carry all the power we need inside ourselves already.'

In a sense, to end this book I simply want to make the same call as Rowling does. She created an extraordinary magical world, a fantasy place that millions have inhabited and learned so much from. But from within that world she offered a lesson: magic has the power to strip us of our humanity, the power to send us mad in a lust for power, the power to drive us towards exclusion of the weak and voiceless.

Harry Potter did the most courageous thing he could. He saw the perils of magic clearly, and pushed beyond it into love.

Rowling's message to the real world is no different. Religions offer a speedy salvation, a powerful set of short cuts to making the world a better place. But if we take up their offers we risk diminishing our humanity and making the world a far *less* good place. What should we do? Rowling never calls for a denial of magic, simply for a renunciation, a sacrifice, the laying down of a potent art, the breaking of a powerful staff. Why? Because if we truly want to make the world better we will have to remake it slowly, carefully, and do so with the love that we carry within us from the parent who laid down their life for us and is, for now, no more.

'After magic,' Prospero's words thus becomes ours, our way to walk front-stage, abjure magic and commit to a justice that we work with our hands together saying:

> *'Now my charms are all o'erthrown*
> *what strength I have's mine own.'*

Or, put in the Cleveland vernacular, it's for us to yell these great words of Harvey Pekar's that might yet bring splendour back to America and beyond:

> *'I ain't no superhero lady,*
> *I'm just a kid from the neighbourhood!'*

New York - London - Pickwell, February 2013

With thanks to LC for showing me Harry
and sharing so much good Will.

And, as ever, to @hauntdgographis
whose courage in dying 'after magic'
continues to inspire so many to live.

Made in the USA
Lexington, KY
03 June 2013